Ancient Remedies Revived

Table of Contents

Introduction to Natural Healing

Understanding Natural Healing: A Historical Perspective

Natural healing, often referred to as traditional or alternative medicine, has deep roots stretching back thousands of years. This practice, which encompasses the use of herbs, plants, and natural elements to treat ailments, is a testament to humanity's intrinsic connection to the natural world. By exploring its historical perspective, we gain insights into how ancient civilizations relied on nature's bounty to promote health and wellness—a tradition that continues to influence modern approaches to medicine.

The Beginnings of Natural Healing

The origins of natural healing can be traced back to prehistoric times when early humans relied on trial and error to discover which plants were beneficial and which were harmful. Archaeological evidence suggests that even Neanderthals used plants like yarrow and chamomile, indicating an early understanding of herbal medicine. As these early societies evolved, so did their knowledge of natural healing, leading to the development of sophisticated herbal practices.

Ancient Civilizations and Their Healing Traditions

- **Egyptian Medicine**: The ancient Egyptians are among the earliest civilizations to document their medical practices. They believed in a holistic approach to health, where physical, spiritual, and emotional well-being were interconnected. The Ebers Papyrus, dating back to around 1550 BCE, is one of the oldest medical texts in existence and includes numerous herbal remedies still in use today, such as garlic for heart health and aloe vera for skin conditions.

- **Traditional Chinese Medicine (TCM)**: Originating over 2,500 years ago, TCM is rooted in the Taoist philosophy of balance and harmony, particularly the balance between yin and yang. Herbal medicine, acupuncture, and qigong are central components of TCM. Herbs like ginseng, ginger, and licorice have been used for centuries to treat a variety of conditions, and their efficacy is supported by modern research.

- **Ayurveda in India**: Ayurveda, which means "the science of life," is a system of medicine that has been practiced in India for over 3,000 years. It focuses on the balance of the body's doshas (vata, pitta, and kapha) and uses herbs, diet, and lifestyle changes to maintain health. Ayurvedic texts like the Charaka Samhita and

Sushruta Samhita describe detailed herbal formulations and treatment protocols that are still relevant today.

- **Greek and Roman Medicine**: The Greeks and Romans made significant contributions to natural healing, with figures like Hippocrates, often called the "Father of Medicine," advocating for the use of diet, exercise, and herbal remedies. Galen, a prominent Roman physician, compiled extensive writings on the medicinal properties of plants. The Greco-Roman tradition laid the groundwork for Western herbalism, influencing the development of modern pharmacology.

Indigenous Healing Practices

Across the world, indigenous cultures developed their own healing traditions, often passed down through generations by oral tradition.

- **Native American Medicine**: Indigenous tribes in North America used a wide variety of plants for medicinal purposes. For example, willow bark, a precursor to aspirin, was used for pain relief, while echinacea was used to boost the immune system. These remedies were often part of a spiritual practice that emphasized the connection between the individual and the natural world.

- **African Traditional Medicine**: African traditional healers, or shamans, employed a deep understanding of the medicinal properties of local plants, as well as spiritual practices, to treat ailments. Plants like the African potato and devil's claw have been used for centuries to treat conditions such as inflammation and arthritis, and their use is now being validated by scientific research.

The Middle Ages and the Renaissance

During the Middle Ages, herbal medicine was preserved and practiced primarily in monasteries, where monks maintained herb gardens and transcribed ancient texts. The Renaissance period saw a revival of interest in classical texts and the natural sciences, leading to the publication of important herbal guides, such as Nicholas Culpeper's *The English Physician*, which democratized medical knowledge by making it accessible to the general public.

The Decline and Resurgence of Natural Healing

With the advent of the Industrial Revolution and the rise of modern medicine in the 19th and 20th centuries, natural healing practices were often dismissed as unscientific. The development of synthetic drugs and a more mechanistic view of the human body led to the marginalization of traditional practices. However, the latter half of the 20th century witnessed a resurgence of interest in natural remedies, driven by a growing awareness of the side effects of pharmaceuticals, a desire for holistic health, and the rediscovery of ancient wisdom.

Natural Healing Today

In the 21st century, natural healing has re-emerged as a complementary and integrative approach to health care. Modern practitioners of natural medicine blend ancient practices with contemporary scientific research to create treatments that are both effective and respectful of the body's natural processes. This revival is not just a trend, but a continuation of a long history of seeking balance, wellness, and harmony with nature.

Understanding the historical perspective of natural healing allows us to appreciate the depth and richness of this tradition. It also provides a foundation for exploring how ancient remedies can be revived and adapted for use in our modern world, offering a holistic approach to health that honors the wisdom of the past.

The Revival of Ancient Remedies in Modern Times

In recent decades, there has been a significant resurgence in the use of ancient remedies as people increasingly seek natural alternatives to conventional medicine. This revival is driven by a combination of cultural, scientific, and societal factors, reflecting a growing appreciation for the holistic approaches that have been used for centuries to promote health and well-being.

The Shift Towards Natural Healing

The late 20th and early 21st centuries have seen a shift in public perception towards natural healing methods. Several factors have contributed to this revival:

- **Health and Wellness Trends**: A broader movement towards holistic health and wellness has led many individuals to explore natural remedies as part of a lifestyle that emphasizes balance, prevention, and personal empowerment.

- **Skepticism of Pharmaceuticals**: Concerns over the side effects of pharmaceuticals, the over-prescription of medications, and the influence of the pharmaceutical industry have led many to seek alternatives that are perceived as safer and more in harmony with the body's natural processes.

- **Cultural Reconnection**: For many, the revival of ancient remedies is also a way of reconnecting with cultural heritage and traditional practices that have been overshadowed by modern medicine. Indigenous and cultural groups are reclaiming their traditional knowledge as part of a broader resurgence of cultural identity.

The Role of Scientific Validation

A crucial factor in the revival of ancient remedies has been the growing body of scientific research validating their efficacy. Modern science has begun to explore the biochemical mechanisms underlying the therapeutic effects of many traditional herbs and treatments.

- **Phytochemicals and Active Compounds**: Research into the active compounds found in medicinal plants has shed light on why these remedies have been effective for centuries. For example, curcumin in turmeric is now recognized for its potent anti-inflammatory properties, and the antioxidant effects of polyphenols in green tea are well-documented.

- **Clinical Trials and Studies**: Increasingly, natural remedies are being subjected to rigorous clinical trials, providing empirical evidence of their benefits. Studies on herbs like echinacea for immune support, St. John's wort for depression, and ginger for nausea have validated their traditional uses.

- **Integrative Medicine**: The rise of integrative medicine, which combines conventional and alternative approaches, has played a significant role in the revival of ancient remedies. Integrative medicine practitioners often use evidence-based natural therapies alongside conventional treatments, providing a holistic approach to patient care.

The Influence of Globalization and Information Access

Globalization has played a pivotal role in spreading knowledge about ancient remedies across cultures and borders. As the world becomes more interconnected, the exchange of medical traditions has led to the blending and adaptation of ancient practices.

- **The Internet and Social Media**: The internet has democratized access to information about natural healing, allowing people to explore and share traditional remedies from around the world. Social media platforms and wellness blogs have popularized the use of ancient herbs, oils, and holistic practices, bringing them into mainstream awareness.

- **Herbal Supplements and Natural Products Market**: The market for herbal supplements and natural products has expanded dramatically, making it easier for consumers to access ancient remedies. This market growth reflects both consumer demand and a recognition by the industry of the value of traditional knowledge.

Modern Applications of Ancient Remedies

The revival of ancient remedies is not just about returning to old practices; it's also about innovatively adapting these traditions for modern use.

- **Adaptogenic Herbs**: Adaptogens like ashwagandha, rhodiola, and holy basil are experiencing renewed popularity for their ability to help the body adapt to stress and maintain balance. These herbs are now often incorporated into modern health products, including supplements, teas, and functional foods.

- **Essential Oils**: Aromatherapy, using essential oils like lavender, eucalyptus, and frankincense, has seen a resurgence as people seek natural ways to support emotional and physical well-being. These oils, extracted from plants, are used in various forms, from diffusers to topical applications.

- **Fermented Foods and Probiotics**: Ancient practices like fermenting foods, which have been used for centuries to preserve food and enhance its nutritional value, are being embraced in the modern diet for their probiotic benefits. Foods like kefir, kimchi, and sauerkraut are now celebrated for their ability to support gut health.

Challenges and Considerations

While the revival of ancient remedies offers many benefits, it also comes with challenges and considerations that need to be addressed:

- **Quality Control and Standardization**: Ensuring the quality and consistency of herbal products is crucial, as variations in preparation and potency can affect efficacy. Modern herbalism requires rigorous standards for cultivation, harvesting, and processing to ensure safety and effectiveness.

- **Ethical Sourcing and Sustainability**: The increasing demand for traditional herbs and remedies raises concerns about overharvesting and the sustainability of these resources. Ethical sourcing practices are essential to protect biodiversity and the communities that rely on these plants for their livelihood.

- **Integration with Modern Medicine**: The integration of ancient remedies with conventional medical practices requires careful consideration, especially regarding potential interactions between herbs and pharmaceuticals. Educating both practitioners and patients about these interactions is vital for safe and effective use.

The Future of Ancient Remedies in Modern Health Care

The revival of ancient remedies is likely to continue growing as people seek more natural and holistic approaches to health. As scientific research continues to validate traditional practices and integrative medicine becomes more mainstream, these ancient remedies will play an increasingly important role in modern health care.

This resurgence is not just a trend but part of a broader movement towards reclaiming and respecting the wisdom of the past. By blending the old with the new, we can create a more balanced and inclusive approach to health that honors the traditions of our ancestors while embracing the advances of modern science.

The Science Behind Natural Remedies

The Intersection of Tradition and Science

The intersection of tradition and science in the realm of natural healing is a fascinating convergence of ancient wisdom and modern research. While traditional medicine has been practiced for thousands of years, often based on empirical knowledge and cultural beliefs, science offers a framework to understand and validate these practices through rigorous study and experimentation. This chapter explores how these two worlds come together to enrich our understanding of natural remedies, making them more accessible and acceptable in contemporary health care.

The Legacy of Traditional Medicine

Traditional medicine encompasses a wide range of practices rooted in the cultural and spiritual beliefs of different civilizations. These practices, which include herbal medicine, acupuncture, Ayurveda, and more, have been passed down through generations and are based on the observation of nature and the human body.

- **Holistic Approach**: Traditional medicine typically adopts a holistic approach, viewing the body as an interconnected system where physical, mental, and spiritual health are intertwined. Remedies are often designed to restore balance and harmony within the body, addressing the root causes of illness rather than just the symptoms.

- **Empirical Knowledge**: Over centuries, traditional healers accumulated empirical knowledge by observing the effects of various herbs, diets, and lifestyle practices on health. This knowledge was shared and refined within communities, leading to the development of sophisticated systems of medicine that are still in use today.

- **Cultural Significance**: Traditional remedies are often deeply embedded in cultural practices and beliefs, reflecting a community's relationship with the environment and its understanding of health and disease. These remedies carry not just medicinal value but also cultural identity and heritage.

The Role of Modern Science

Modern science, with its emphasis on evidence-based medicine, seeks to understand the mechanisms behind traditional remedies and validate their efficacy through systematic study.

- **Pharmacological Research**: One of the primary ways science intersects with tradition is through pharmacological research, which identifies and isolates active compounds in medicinal plants. This research helps explain why certain herbs are effective and can lead to the development of new drugs derived from these natural sources. For example, the discovery of aspirin was based on the active compound salicin found in willow bark, a traditional remedy for pain relief.

- **Clinical Trials and Studies**: Clinical trials are conducted to test the safety and effectiveness of traditional remedies in controlled environments. These studies provide quantitative data that can support the use of natural remedies in modern medicine. For instance, clinical trials have demonstrated the efficacy of St. John's wort in treating mild to moderate depression, validating its long-standing use in traditional European medicine.

- **Integrative Medicine**: The field of integrative medicine blends conventional medical treatments with complementary therapies, including traditional remedies. By combining the best of both worlds, integrative medicine offers a more comprehensive approach to health care that respects the insights of tradition while adhering to scientific standards.

Bridging the Gap Between Tradition and Science

The collaboration between traditional knowledge and modern science is essential for advancing our understanding of natural remedies and ensuring their safe and effective use.

- **Ethnopharmacology**: This scientific discipline studies the traditional use of medicinal plants and natural products in various cultures. Ethnopharmacologists work closely with indigenous communities to document traditional knowledge and investigate the pharmacological properties of natural remedies. This collaboration not only preserves cultural heritage but also contributes to the discovery of new therapeutic agents.

- **Standardization and Quality Control**: One of the challenges of integrating traditional remedies into modern medicine is ensuring consistency in quality and potency. Science plays a crucial role in developing standardized extraction methods, dosage forms, and quality control measures to ensure that natural remedies are safe and effective.

- **Respecting Indigenous Knowledge**: It's important to recognize and respect the intellectual property rights of indigenous communities who have developed and maintained traditional knowledge over centuries. Ethical considerations in the commercialization of traditional remedies include fair compensation and acknowledgment of the source communities.

Case Studies: Tradition Meets Science

- **Turmeric and Curcumin**: Turmeric, a staple in Ayurvedic medicine, has been used for thousands of years to treat inflammation and other ailments. Modern science has identified curcumin, a compound in turmeric, as the source of its anti-inflammatory and antioxidant properties. Extensive research has led to curcumin being studied and used in modern medicine for conditions such as arthritis and cancer.

- **Ginkgo Biloba**: Ginkgo biloba, used in traditional Chinese medicine for centuries to improve memory and circulation, has been the subject of numerous scientific studies. These studies have shown that ginkgo may have neuroprotective effects and could be beneficial in treating cognitive decline, although more research is needed to fully understand its potential.

- **Acupuncture**: Acupuncture, an ancient Chinese practice, has been increasingly studied in the West. While originally rooted in the concept of balancing the body's energy flow (Qi), modern studies have explored its effects on the nervous system, endorphin release, and blood flow. The World Health Organization recognizes acupuncture as effective for a variety of conditions, bridging the gap between traditional practice and scientific validation.

The Future of Natural Healing

The ongoing dialogue between tradition and science holds great promise for the future of natural healing. As science continues to explore the biochemical and physiological effects of traditional remedies, and as traditional medicine practitioners embrace scientific validation, we are likely to see a more integrative approach to health care.

- **Personalized Medicine**: The future may also see more personalized approaches to natural healing, where genetic, environmental, and lifestyle factors are considered in tailoring remedies to individual needs. This approach would combine the wisdom of traditional practices with the precision of modern science.

- **Sustainable Practices**: As the popularity of natural remedies grows, there is also an increased focus on sustainable harvesting and ethical sourcing. Science and tradition must work together to ensure that the revival of ancient remedies does not come at the cost of environmental degradation or cultural exploitation.

Research Supporting the Efficacy of Herbal Medicine

Herbal medicine, an integral part of many traditional health systems, is increasingly being validated through scientific research. This growing body of evidence supports the use of various herbs for a wide range of health conditions, confirming what many cultures have known for centuries—that plants and their extracts can have powerful therapeutic effects. This chapter explores the research supporting the efficacy of herbal medicine, highlighting key studies and findings that underscore the role of herbs in modern health care.

The Rise of Evidence-Based Herbal Medicine

Evidence-based herbal medicine combines traditional knowledge with scientific research to assess the safety and efficacy of herbal remedies. This approach involves rigorous testing through clinical trials, observational studies, and laboratory research to provide reliable data on the benefits and risks of herbal treatments.

- **Clinical Trials**: Clinical trials are the gold standard for evaluating the effectiveness of herbal remedies. These studies involve administering herbal treatments to participants in a controlled setting and measuring outcomes against a placebo or standard treatment. Positive results from well-designed trials can lead to the integration of herbal remedies into mainstream medical practice.

- **Systematic Reviews and Meta-Analyses**: Systematic reviews and meta-analyses synthesize findings from multiple studies to provide a comprehensive assessment of the efficacy and safety of herbal remedies. These reviews help to identify patterns, resolve inconsistencies, and provide a clearer picture of how well a remedy works.

Key Studies and Findings

Here are some notable examples of research that supports the efficacy of herbal medicine:

- **Echinacea for Immune Support**: Echinacea is widely used to prevent and treat colds and other respiratory infections. Research has shown that echinacea can stimulate the immune system, reducing the severity and duration of cold symptoms. A systematic review of clinical trials found that echinacea extracts could reduce the risk of developing a cold by about 10-20% and shorten its duration by 1-2 days.

- **St. John's Wort for Depression**: St. John's wort has been used for centuries to treat mild to moderate depression. Numerous studies have confirmed its efficacy, with clinical trials showing that it can be as effective as standard antidepressant medications for some individuals. A meta-analysis of 29 studies found that St. John's wort was significantly more effective than a placebo and comparable to conventional antidepressants in reducing symptoms of depression.

- **Ginger for Nausea and Digestive Health**: Ginger is a well-known remedy for nausea and digestive discomfort. Clinical studies have demonstrated its effectiveness in treating nausea associated with pregnancy, chemotherapy, and motion sickness. Research shows that ginger reduces nausea and vomiting through its anti-inflammatory and prokinetic effects, which help to stabilize the digestive system.

- **Turmeric and Curcumin for Inflammation**: Turmeric contains curcumin, a compound with strong anti-inflammatory and antioxidant properties. Research has shown that curcumin can be effective in managing chronic inflammatory conditions such as arthritis and inflammatory bowel disease. Studies have found that curcumin can reduce inflammation and pain in conditions like osteoarthritis and rheumatoid arthritis, often with fewer side effects compared to conventional anti-inflammatory drugs.

- **Garlic for Cardiovascular Health**: Garlic has long been used for its cardiovascular benefits, including lowering blood pressure and cholesterol levels. Research supports these uses, with studies showing that garlic supplements can lead to modest reductions in blood pressure and improvements in lipid profiles. A meta-analysis of clinical trials found that garlic supplementation could reduce total cholesterol levels by 10-15% and systolic blood pressure by about 8-10 mmHg.

Mechanisms of Action

Understanding the mechanisms by which herbal remedies exert their effects is crucial for validating their use. Research often focuses on identifying the active compounds in herbs and how they interact with biological systems.

- **Phytochemicals**: Phytochemicals are naturally occurring compounds in plants that contribute to their therapeutic effects. For example, the flavonoids in green tea have antioxidant properties that protect cells from damage, while the saponins in ginseng may enhance physical and mental performance.

- **Pharmacodynamics**: Studies investigate how herbal compounds affect the body at the molecular level. For instance, research on curcumin has explored its ability to modulate inflammatory pathways and inhibit pro-inflammatory cytokines, providing insight into its role in managing chronic inflammation.

- **Pharmacokinetics**: Research also examines how herbal compounds are absorbed, distributed, metabolized, and excreted by the body. This information helps to determine the appropriate dosage and potential interactions with other medications.

Challenges and Considerations

While the evidence supporting herbal medicine is growing, several challenges and considerations must be addressed:

- **Standardization and Quality Control**: One of the challenges in herbal medicine research is ensuring the consistency and quality of herbal products. Variability in plant sources, preparation methods, and dosage can affect the efficacy and safety of herbal remedies. Standardization and quality control are essential for reliable research outcomes and safe use.

- **Herb-Drug Interactions**: Herbal remedies can interact with prescription medications, potentially affecting their efficacy or causing adverse effects. Research into herb-drug interactions is important for understanding potential risks and ensuring safe use in combination with conventional treatments.

- **Ethical and Cultural Considerations**: Research on traditional herbal remedies must be conducted with respect for the cultural and intellectual property rights of indigenous communities. Ethical considerations include obtaining informed consent and providing fair compensation for the use of traditional knowledge.

The Future of Herbal Medicine Research

The future of herbal medicine research looks promising, with continued advancements in scientific techniques and a growing recognition of the value of traditional remedies. Key areas of focus include:

- **Personalized Herbal Medicine**: Research is increasingly exploring how individual genetic, environmental, and lifestyle factors influence the efficacy of herbal remedies. Personalized approaches could enhance the effectiveness of treatments and minimize adverse effects.

- **Integrative Approaches**: Combining herbal medicine with conventional treatments and other complementary therapies is an area of active research. Integrative approaches aim to provide comprehensive care that leverages the strengths of both traditional and modern practices.

- **Innovations in Delivery Systems**: Advances in technology are leading to innovations in the delivery systems of herbal remedies, such as nano-formulations and advanced extraction methods. These innovations could enhance the bioavailability and effectiveness of herbal treatments.

The Role of Phytochemicals in Healing

Phytochemicals are natural compounds found in plants that contribute to their color, flavor, and disease resistance. These compounds have been recognized for their potential health benefits, and research has increasingly focused on their role in healing and disease prevention. This chapter explores the significance of phytochemicals in natural medicine, detailing their mechanisms of action, therapeutic effects, and potential applications in health care.

Understanding Phytochemicals

Phytochemicals are categorized into several classes, each with unique properties and effects on the body. Some of the major classes of phytochemicals include:

- **Flavonoids**: A diverse group of compounds responsible for the color of many fruits, vegetables, and flowers. Flavonoids have been shown to have antioxidant, anti-inflammatory, and antimicrobial properties. Examples include quercetin in apples and catechins in green tea.

- **Phenolic Acids**: These compounds are found in a variety of plant foods and are known for their antioxidant and anti-inflammatory effects. Cinnamic acid, found in cinnamon, and caffeic acid, found in coffee, are notable examples.

- **Terpenes**: A large class of phytochemicals that contribute to the aroma and flavor of plants. Terpenes like limonene (found in citrus fruits) and pinene (found in pine) have been studied for their potential anticancer, anti-inflammatory, and antimicrobial effects.

- **Alkaloids**: Nitrogen-containing compounds with various biological activities. Alkaloids such as caffeine (found in coffee) and morphine (derived from the opium poppy) have significant pharmacological effects.

- **Saponins**: Compounds with soap-like properties that can interact with cell membranes. Saponins, found in foods like quinoa and beans, have been studied for their immune-boosting and cholesterol-lowering effects.

- **Glucosinolates**: Compounds found in cruciferous vegetables like broccoli and Brussels sprouts. They are known for their potential anticancer effects through the modulation of detoxification enzymes and antioxidant defense systems.

Mechanisms of Action

Phytochemicals exert their effects through various mechanisms, often involving the modulation of biochemical pathways and cellular processes:

- **Antioxidant Activity**: Many phytochemicals act as antioxidants, neutralizing free radicals and reducing oxidative stress. This action helps protect cells from damage and may reduce the risk of chronic diseases such as cancer and cardiovascular disease.

- **Anti-Inflammatory Effects**: Phytochemicals can modulate inflammatory pathways by inhibiting pro-inflammatory enzymes and cytokines. For instance, curcumin in turmeric and resveratrol in grapes have been shown to reduce inflammation and improve symptoms of inflammatory conditions.

- **Immune Modulation**: Some phytochemicals enhance or regulate the immune system, improving the body's ability to fight infections and diseases. Echinacea and astragalus, for example, are known for their immune-boosting properties.

- **Hormonal Regulation**: Certain phytochemicals can influence hormonal activity, which can be beneficial in managing conditions like hormonal imbalances and certain types of cancer. Phytoestrogens found in soybeans can mimic or modulate estrogen activity in the body.

- **Antimicrobial Activity**: Many phytochemicals have antimicrobial properties, inhibiting the growth of bacteria, viruses, and fungi. Garlic, for example, contains allicin, which has been shown to have antibacterial and antiviral effects.

Health Benefits and Applications

Phytochemicals have been linked to various health benefits, supported by both traditional use and modern research:

- **Cardiovascular Health**: Phytochemicals like flavonoids and phenolic acids have been shown to improve cardiovascular health by reducing blood pressure, lowering cholesterol levels, and preventing arterial plaque formation. The consumption of foods rich in these compounds, such as berries and dark chocolate, is associated with a lower risk of heart disease.

- **Cancer Prevention**: Many phytochemicals possess anticancer properties through mechanisms such as detoxification, apoptosis (programmed cell death), and inhibition of tumor growth. Cruciferous vegetables, rich in glucosinolates, and foods containing lycopene (like tomatoes) have been studied for their cancer-preventive effects.

- **Cognitive Health**: Phytochemicals like curcumin and resveratrol have been investigated for their potential to protect against neurodegenerative diseases. Their antioxidant and anti-inflammatory properties may help reduce cognitive decline and support brain health.

- **Digestive Health**: Phytochemicals such as fiber, saponins, and polyphenols promote digestive health by supporting gut microbiota, reducing inflammation, and enhancing digestion. Foods rich in these compounds, like legumes and whole grains, contribute to a healthy digestive system.

- **Skin Health**: Phytochemicals can also benefit skin health by protecting against oxidative damage, reducing inflammation, and promoting wound healing. Ingredients like vitamin C (found in citrus fruits) and polyphenols (found in green tea) are commonly used in skincare products for their protective and rejuvenating effects.

Challenges and Considerations

While phytochemicals offer numerous health benefits, there are several challenges and considerations to keep in mind:

- **Bioavailability**: The effectiveness of phytochemicals depends on their bioavailability, which is the degree to which they are absorbed and utilized by the body. Factors such as food preparation, individual metabolism, and interactions with other nutrients can influence bioavailability.

- **Standardization and Dosage**: Ensuring consistent quality and dosage of phytochemical-rich supplements is essential for reliable health outcomes. Variability in the concentration of active compounds can affect the efficacy and safety of herbal products.

- **Interactions with Medications**: Phytochemicals can interact with prescription medications, potentially affecting their efficacy or causing adverse effects. It is important to consider these interactions when using herbal remedies, especially for individuals taking multiple medications.

- **Ethical and Environmental Concerns**: The cultivation and harvesting of plants for phytochemical extraction must be done sustainably and ethically. Overharvesting and environmental degradation can impact the availability of medicinal plants and their effectiveness.

Future Directions

Research into phytochemicals continues to expand, with ongoing studies exploring their full potential and applications in health care. Future directions include:

- **Personalized Nutrition**: Investigating how individual genetic and health profiles affect the response to phytochemicals could lead to more personalized and effective dietary recommendations and supplements.

- **Innovative Delivery Systems**: Advances in technology may lead to new methods for enhancing the bioavailability and targeted delivery of phytochemicals, improving their therapeutic potential.

- **Integration with Conventional Medicine**: Exploring how phytochemicals can complement conventional treatments and contribute to integrative health care approaches holds promise for enhancing patient outcomes and expanding treatment options.

In conclusion, phytochemicals play a significant role in healing and health promotion, with scientific research increasingly validating their benefits. By understanding their mechanisms of action and applications, we can harness the power of these natural compounds to support overall health and well-being.

Understanding the Body's Natural Healing Mechanisms

The human body is equipped with sophisticated systems designed to maintain health and repair itself. These natural healing mechanisms are essential for recovery from injury, infection, and disease, and they work in concert to restore balance and function. This chapter explores these mechanisms, highlighting how the body detects and responds to various challenges, and how natural healing can be supported and enhanced through lifestyle choices and complementary therapies.

The Immune System: The Body's Defense Network

The immune system is a complex network of cells, tissues, and organs that work together to defend the body against pathogens such as bacteria, viruses, fungi, and parasites.

- **Innate Immunity**: This is the body's first line of defense and includes physical barriers (like the skin and mucous membranes) and immune cells (such as macrophages and neutrophils) that respond quickly to potential threats. Innate immunity provides a broad, non-specific response to infections and injuries.

- **Adaptive Immunity**: This system develops over time and provides a specific response to particular pathogens. It involves lymphocytes, such as T cells and B cells, which recognize and remember specific antigens. This memory allows for a faster and more efficient response upon subsequent exposures to the same pathogen.

- **Inflammatory Response**: Inflammation is a key component of the immune response, characterized by redness, heat, swelling, and pain at the site of injury or infection. It helps to eliminate pathogens and initiate repair. However, chronic inflammation can lead to tissue damage and disease, so regulating this response is crucial for overall health.

The Healing Process: Repair and Regeneration

The healing process involves several stages, each essential for restoring tissue integrity and function:

- **Hemostasis**: This initial stage begins immediately after an injury. Blood vessels constrict to reduce bleeding, and platelets form a clot to seal the wound. This clot also releases factors that promote healing.

- **Inflammation**: Following hemostasis, inflammation occurs to remove debris and pathogens. White blood cells migrate to the site of injury, releasing chemicals that help clear out damaged cells and microbes.

- **Proliferation**: During this phase, new tissue is formed. This includes the proliferation of fibroblasts (which produce collagen and extracellular matrix) and the formation of new blood vessels (angiogenesis) to supply nutrients and oxygen to the healing tissue.

- **Maturation**: The final stage involves the remodeling of the new tissue. Collagen fibers are reorganized, and the tissue gains strength and elasticity. This phase can last for months to years, depending on the severity of the injury.

The Role of Genetics in Healing

Genetics plays a significant role in determining the efficiency and effectiveness of the body's healing processes. Genetic factors can influence:

- **Wound Healing**: Variations in genes related to collagen production, inflammation, and immune response can affect how quickly and effectively wounds heal.

- **Disease Susceptibility**: Genetic predispositions can impact susceptibility to certain diseases and the body's ability to respond to infections or injuries.

- **Pharmacogenomics**: Individual genetic variations can affect how people respond to medications, including those used to support healing and manage pain. This field, known as pharmacogenomics, helps tailor treatments based on genetic profiles.

The Impact of Lifestyle on Natural Healing

Lifestyle choices can significantly influence the body's natural healing mechanisms. Factors such as diet, exercise, sleep, and stress management play crucial roles in maintaining and enhancing the body's ability to heal.

- **Nutrition**: Adequate nutrition provides the essential nutrients and energy needed for the healing process. Vitamins (such as Vitamin C and Vitamin A), minerals (such as zinc and magnesium), and proteins are critical for tissue repair and immune function. A balanced diet rich in fruits, vegetables, whole grains, and lean proteins supports optimal healing.

- **Exercise**: Regular physical activity promotes circulation, which aids in the delivery of nutrients and removal of waste products from the tissues. Exercise also supports immune function and helps reduce inflammation. However, excessive or inappropriate exercise can hinder healing, so a balanced approach is necessary.

- **Sleep**: Quality sleep is vital for recovery and repair. During sleep, the body releases growth hormones and other factors that support tissue regeneration and immune function. Poor sleep can impair these processes and increase susceptibility to illness and injury.

- **Stress Management**: Chronic stress can negatively impact the immune system and healing processes. Stress hormones like cortisol can suppress immune function and increase inflammation. Techniques such as mindfulness, meditation, and relaxation exercises can help manage stress and support overall health.

Complementary Therapies and Natural Healing

Complementary therapies can enhance the body's natural healing mechanisms and support conventional medical treatments:

- **Herbal Medicine**: Many herbs contain compounds that can modulate inflammation, support immune function, and promote tissue repair. Examples include echinacea for immune support, turmeric for its anti-inflammatory properties, and ginseng for overall vitality.

- **Acupuncture**: Traditional Chinese medicine practices like acupuncture can stimulate the body's natural healing processes by improving energy flow (Qi) and promoting balance. Research suggests that acupuncture may help with pain management, inflammation, and overall wellness.

- **Mind-Body Techniques**: Practices such as yoga, Tai Chi, and meditation can support healing by reducing stress, improving mental health, and enhancing physical function. These techniques help balance the mind and body, which can positively influence the body's ability to recover.

- **Physical Therapy**: For musculoskeletal injuries, physical therapy can aid in rehabilitation by improving mobility, strength, and function. Therapists use exercises, manual therapy, and modalities to support the healing process and prevent future injuries.

Challenges and Considerations

While the body's natural healing mechanisms are remarkable, there are challenges and considerations to keep in mind:

- **Chronic Conditions**: Chronic diseases and conditions, such as diabetes and autoimmune disorders, can impair the body's natural healing processes. Managing these conditions effectively is crucial for supporting overall healing and recovery.

- **Age**: Age-related changes in the immune system and tissue repair processes can affect healing. Older adults may experience slower healing and increased susceptibility to infections, requiring tailored interventions to support recovery.

- **Environmental Factors**: Exposure to toxins, pollutants, and environmental stressors can impact the body's ability to heal. Minimizing exposure and promoting a healthy environment can support natural healing.

In conclusion, understanding the body's natural healing mechanisms provides valuable insights into how we can support and enhance these processes. By maintaining a healthy lifestyle, utilizing complementary therapies, and addressing challenges, we can optimize our body's ability to heal and maintain overall health and well-being.

Herbal Synergies: Combining Herbs for Maximum Effect

The Concept of Herbal Synergies

Herbal synergies refer to the enhanced therapeutic effects that occur when multiple herbs are combined in a formula. The idea is that the interactions between different herbs can amplify their individual benefits, create new effects, or reduce potential side effects. This concept is rooted in traditional herbal practices and is increasingly supported by modern research, which explores how combining herbs can optimize their therapeutic potential.

Principles of Herbal Synergies

Understanding herbal synergies involves several key principles:

- **Complementary Actions**: Herbs with complementary actions can work together to address different aspects of a health condition. For example, one herb may have anti-inflammatory properties while another supports immune function, creating a more comprehensive approach to managing inflammation.

- **Enhanced Absorption**: Some herbs can enhance the absorption or bioavailability of others. For instance, combining herbs that contain compounds to improve digestion can help in the better absorption of nutrients and active compounds from other herbs.

- **Balancing Effects**: Combining herbs can help balance their effects, mitigating potential side effects or counteracting undesired actions. For example, a strong stimulant herb might be paired with a calming herb to balance its stimulating effects and reduce the risk of overstimulation.

- **Synergistic Effects**: Synergistic interactions occur when the combined effects of herbs are greater than the sum of their individual effects. This can result in enhanced therapeutic outcomes, such as increased efficacy or reduced dosage requirements.

Examples of Herbal Synergies

Here are some examples of how combining herbs can create effective synergies:

- **Immune Support**: A formula combining echinacea, known for its immune-stimulating properties, with elderberry, which has antiviral effects, can provide a comprehensive approach to preventing and managing colds and flu. Echinacea boosts the immune system's ability to fight infections, while elderberry helps combat the viruses that cause respiratory illnesses.

- **Digestive Health**: Combining ginger, which aids digestion and reduces nausea, with peppermint, which soothes the digestive tract and relieves bloating, can create a synergistic effect that addresses multiple aspects of digestive discomfort. Ginger stimulates digestive enzymes, while peppermint relaxes the muscles of the gastrointestinal tract.

- **Anti-Inflammatory Blends**: Turmeric, with its potent anti-inflammatory properties due to curcumin, can be combined with boswellia, another anti-inflammatory herb, to enhance overall anti-inflammatory effects. This combination can be more effective for managing chronic inflammatory conditions compared to using either herb alone.

- **Sleep and Relaxation**: A blend of valerian root, which promotes relaxation and improves sleep quality, and chamomile, known for its calming effects, can be used to support better sleep and reduce insomnia. Valerian helps to initiate and maintain sleep, while chamomile enhances relaxation and reduces anxiety.

Creating Balanced Herbal Blends

To create effective herbal blends, several factors need to be considered:

- **Herb Selection**: Choose herbs that complement each other's actions and address different aspects of the health condition. Ensure that the herbs chosen have a history of safe use and are appropriate for the intended purpose.

- **Dosage and Proportions**: Determine the appropriate dosage and proportions for each herb based on their individual properties and interactions. This may involve consulting herbal literature, traditional practices, or clinical research to ensure efficacy and safety.

- **Preparation Methods**: The method of preparation (e.g., teas, tinctures, capsules) can influence the effectiveness of the herbal blend. Consider the best preparation method for each herb and the desired therapeutic effect.

- **Safety and Interactions**: Be mindful of potential interactions between herbs and other medications or health conditions. Ensure that the combination of herbs does not cause adverse effects or interfere with conventional treatments.

Research and Evidence

Modern research is increasingly exploring the concept of herbal synergies. Some studies have focused on:

- **Pharmacokinetics**: Research on how herbal combinations affect the absorption, metabolism, and elimination of active compounds. For example, studies have investigated how combining certain herbs can enhance or inhibit the bioavailability of specific compounds.

- **Clinical Trials**: Clinical trials that evaluate the efficacy of herbal blends for specific health conditions. These studies provide evidence on how combinations of herbs perform in managing conditions such as chronic pain, cardiovascular health, and mental well-being.

- **Traditional Knowledge**: The integration of traditional herbal knowledge with scientific research to validate and optimize herbal combinations. Traditional practices often provide valuable insights into effective herbal synergies that can be further explored through modern research.

Practical Considerations

When creating and using herbal blends, consider the following practical aspects:

- **Consultation with Experts**: Consulting with a qualified herbalist or healthcare provider can provide guidance on selecting and using herbal combinations safely and effectively.

- **Quality and Source**: Use high-quality herbs from reputable sources to ensure purity and potency. The quality of herbs can significantly impact the effectiveness of herbal blends.

- **Personalization**: Herbal blends should be tailored to individual needs and health conditions. Personal factors such as age, health status, and specific symptoms can influence the choice and formulation of herbal combinations.

The concept of herbal synergies offers a valuable approach to enhancing the effectiveness of herbal remedies. By understanding how different herbs interact and complement each other, practitioners can create more powerful and balanced formulations that address a range of health conditions. Continued research and exploration of herbal synergies will contribute to optimizing natural healing practices and integrating them effectively into modern health care.

Creating Balanced Herbal Blends

Creating balanced herbal blends involves combining multiple herbs to enhance their therapeutic effects while minimizing potential side effects. The goal is to craft a formula that synergistically addresses specific health concerns, leverages the complementary properties of each herb, and maintains safety and efficacy. This process requires a thoughtful approach to herb selection, dosage, preparation, and evaluation.

Key Considerations for Crafting Herbal Blends

1. **Identify the Health Objective**: Define the specific health issue or condition you aim to address with the herbal blend. Whether it's managing stress, improving digestion, or supporting immune health, having a clear objective will guide your herb selection and formulation process.

2. **Select Complementary Herbs**: Choose herbs that complement each other's actions and contribute to the desired therapeutic effect. Consider the following aspects when selecting herbs:

   o **Actions and Properties**: Identify herbs with actions that align with your health objective. For example, for digestive support, you might choose herbs that promote digestion, soothe the gut, and relieve discomfort.

   o **Synergistic Effects**: Look for herbs that work together to enhance each other's effects. For instance, combining a stimulating herb with a calming herb can create a balanced effect, such as reducing anxiety while maintaining mental alertness.

   o **Potential Interactions**: Be aware of how different herbs might interact with each other. Some herbs may potentiate each other's effects, while others may counteract or diminish them.

3. **Determine Dosage and Proportions**: The effectiveness of a herbal blend depends on the appropriate dosage and proportions of each herb. Consider:

   o **Dosage**: Research the recommended dosages for each herb based on their intended use and therapeutic effects. Dosages can vary depending on the form of the herb (e.g., tincture, tea, capsule).

   o **Proportions**: Adjust the proportions of each herb in the blend to achieve a balanced formula. Some herbs may need to be used in higher amounts for their primary effects, while others may be included in smaller quantities to support or balance the formula.

4. **Choose the Right Preparation Method**: The method of preparation can impact the effectiveness of the herbal blend. Common preparation methods include:

   o **Teas and Infusions**: Suitable for herbs with water-soluble compounds. Steeping herbs in hot water extracts their active ingredients.

   o **Tinctures**: Alcohol-based extracts that concentrate the active compounds of herbs. Tinctures are effective for herbs with both water-soluble and alcohol-soluble compounds.

   o **Capsules and Tablets**: Convenient for precise dosing and for herbs that may be less palatable in other forms.

   o **Ointments and Salves**: Used for topical applications to address skin conditions or localized pain.

5. **Evaluate Safety and Potential Side Effects**: Ensure that the herbal blend is safe for the intended use. Consider:

   o **Individual Sensitivities**: Be mindful of any allergies or sensitivities to specific herbs.

   o **Interactions with Medications**: Check for potential interactions between the herbs in the blend and any prescription or over-the-counter medications.

   o **Health Conditions**: Consider any pre-existing health conditions that might affect the safety or efficacy of the herbal blend.

6. **Test and Adjust**: Once the herbal blend is formulated, it's important to test its effectiveness and adjust as needed. This may involve:

   o **Initial Testing**: Start with a small batch and observe the effects. Note any changes in symptoms or overall well-being.

   o **Adjustments**: Based on the initial testing, adjust the herb proportions or dosage if necessary to achieve the desired effects.

Example Formulations

1. **Stress and Anxiety Relief Blend**:

   o **Ashwagandha** (Withania somnifera): Known for its adaptogenic properties that help the body manage stress.

   o **Chamomile** (Matricaria chamomilla): Calms the nervous system and promotes relaxation.

- **Lavender** (Lavandula angustifolia): Reduces anxiety and supports restful sleep.

Preparation: Combine equal parts of dried ashwagandha, chamomile, and lavender in a tea blend. Steep 1-2 teaspoons of the mixture in hot water for 10 minutes.

2. **Digestive Support Blend**:
   - **Ginger** (Zingiber officinale): Aids digestion and relieves nausea.
   - **Peppermint** (Mentha piperita): Soothes the digestive tract and reduces bloating.
   - **Fennel** (Foeniculum vulgare): Supports digestion and alleviates gas.

Preparation: Create a tincture by combining equal parts of ginger, peppermint, and fennel in a 1:5 ratio with alcohol. Take 20-30 drops of the tincture before meals.

3. **Anti-Inflammatory Blend**:
   - **Turmeric** (Curcuma longa): Contains curcumin, which has powerful anti-inflammatory effects.
   - **Boswellia** (Boswellia serrata): Supports joint health and reduces inflammation.
   - **Ginger** (Zingiber officinale): Enhances the anti-inflammatory effects of the blend.

Preparation: Mix dried turmeric root, boswellia extract, and ginger powder in a 2:1:1 ratio. Encapsulate the blend or add it to smoothies or teas.

Creating balanced herbal blends requires knowledge of herbal properties, careful selection of complementary herbs, and consideration of preparation methods and dosages. By following these guidelines and adjusting based on individual needs and responses, you can craft effective herbal formulas that support various aspects of health and well-being. Continual learning and experimentation, along with consultation with experienced herbalists, can further enhance your ability to create successful and balanced herbal blends.

Case Studies: Effective Herb Combinations for Common Ailments

Case studies offer valuable insights into how herbal combinations can be effectively used to address common health conditions. By examining real-life examples, we can better understand the practical applications of herbal medicine and the outcomes achieved through specific herb blends. Below are several case studies demonstrating effective herb combinations for various ailments.

1. Case Study: Managing Chronic Stress and Anxiety

Patient Background: A 45-year-old woman with a high-stress job reported symptoms of chronic anxiety, including restlessness, difficulty sleeping, and muscle tension. Conventional treatments had provided limited relief, prompting her to explore herbal remedies.

Herbal Combination:

- **Ashwagandha (Withania somnifera)**: An adaptogen known for its stress-reducing and calming effects.
- **Chamomile (Matricaria chamomilla)**: A calming herb that supports relaxation and helps with sleep.
- **Lavender (Lavandula angustifolia)**: Known for its soothing properties and ability to reduce anxiety.

Preparation and Dosage:

- **Tea**: A blend of equal parts of dried ashwagandha, chamomile, and lavender. Steep 1-2 teaspoons of the mixture in hot water for 10 minutes, taken twice daily.
- **Tincture**: Ashwagandha and lavender tinctures, taken 20 drops of each, twice daily.

Outcome: After 6 weeks of using the herbal blend, the patient reported a significant reduction in anxiety symptoms, improved sleep quality, and a greater sense of calm. The herbal regimen was well-tolerated with no adverse effects.

2. Case Study: Easing Digestive Discomfort

Patient Background: A 32-year-old man experienced frequent digestive issues, including bloating, gas, and occasional nausea. He sought a natural remedy to manage these symptoms.

Herbal Combination:

- **Ginger (Zingiber officinale)**: Known for its ability to relieve nausea and support digestion.

- **Peppermint (Mentha piperita)**: Helps to soothe the digestive tract and reduce bloating.

- **Fennel (Foeniculum vulgare)**: Supports digestive health and alleviates gas.

Preparation and Dosage:

- **Tea**: A blend of dried ginger root, peppermint leaves, and fennel seeds, combined in equal parts. Steep 1 teaspoon of the mixture in hot water for 10 minutes, consumed after meals.

- **Tincture**: Ginger and peppermint tinctures, 15-20 drops of each, taken before meals.

Outcome: After 4 weeks, the patient experienced notable improvement in digestive symptoms. Bloating and gas were reduced, and nausea episodes became less frequent. The combination was effective in managing discomfort and enhancing digestive function.

3. Case Study: Supporting Joint Health and Reducing Inflammation

Patient Background: A 60-year-old man with osteoarthritis reported persistent joint pain and stiffness, affecting his mobility and quality of life. He sought a herbal approach to support joint health and reduce inflammation.

Herbal Combination:

- **Turmeric (Curcuma longa)**: Contains curcumin, which has strong anti-inflammatory and analgesic properties.

- **Boswellia (Boswellia serrata)**: Known for its anti-inflammatory effects, particularly beneficial for joint health.

- **Ginger (Zingiber officinale)**: Provides additional anti-inflammatory benefits and helps with joint pain.

Preparation and Dosage:

- **Capsules**: A combination of turmeric extract, boswellia extract, and ginger powder in a 2:1:1 ratio. The patient took 500 mg of the blend twice daily.

- **Tea**: Turmeric and ginger root tea, prepared with 1 teaspoon of each, steeped in hot water for 10 minutes.

Outcome: After 8 weeks, the patient reported a significant reduction in joint pain and stiffness. Improved mobility and decreased reliance on over-the-counter pain medications were noted. The herbal combination provided effective relief with no adverse reactions.

4. Case Study: Enhancing Immune Function

Patient Background: A 40-year-old woman frequently experienced colds and flu, with a history of weakened immune function. She sought to boost her immune system naturally.

Herbal Combination:

- **Echinacea (Echinacea purpurea)**: Known for its immune-stimulating properties, helpful in preventing and managing infections.

- **Elderberry (Sambucus nigra)**: Provides antiviral effects and supports immune response.

- **Astragalus (Astragalus membranaceus)**: An adaptogen that enhances immune function and overall vitality.

Preparation and Dosage:

- **Tincture**: Echinacea, elderberry, and astragalus tinctures, 20 drops of each, taken daily during cold and flu season.

- **Tea**: A blend of dried elderberry and astragalus root, steeped in hot water for 10 minutes, consumed once daily.

Outcome: After 3 months, the patient reported fewer incidences of illness and a stronger immune response. The herbal regimen contributed to improved overall health and resilience to infections.

5. Case Study: Supporting Healthy Sleep Patterns

Patient Background: A 50-year-old man struggled with insomnia and difficulty falling asleep, impacting his overall well-being. He wanted a natural solution to improve his sleep quality.

Herbal Combination:

- **Valerian Root (Valeriana officinalis)**: Known for its sedative properties, aiding in the onset of sleep.

- **Passionflower (Passiflora incarnata)**: Helps reduce anxiety and improve sleep quality.

- **Hops (Humulus lupulus)**: Used to promote relaxation and support sleep.

Preparation and Dosage:

- **Tea**: A blend of valerian root, passionflower, and hops, in equal parts. Steep 1 teaspoon of the mixture in hot water for 10 minutes, taken 30 minutes before bedtime.

- **Tincture**: Valerian and passionflower tinctures, 20 drops of each, taken before sleep.

Outcome: After 6 weeks, the patient experienced improved sleep onset and quality. Nighttime awakenings decreased, and overall sleep satisfaction increased. The herbal blend effectively addressed his insomnia with minimal side effects.

These case studies illustrate the practical application of herbal combinations for managing common health conditions. By thoughtfully selecting and combining herbs, individuals can address specific symptoms and enhance overall well-being. Each case highlights the importance of personalized approaches and the potential benefits of integrating herbal remedies into daily health practices. Always consult with a healthcare provider or qualified herbalist before starting any new herbal regimen, especially if you have underlying health conditions or are taking other medications.

Safety and Precautions in Herb Mixing

When combining herbs to create effective herbal blends, safety and precaution are paramount. While herbal remedies can offer numerous health benefits, improper use or combinations can lead to adverse effects or interactions. Ensuring the safety and efficacy of herbal blends involves careful consideration of herb properties, dosage, preparation methods, and individual health conditions. Here's a comprehensive guide to safely mixing herbs:

1. Understand Herb Interactions

Herb-Herb Interactions:

- **Synergistic Effects**: Some herbs enhance each other's effects. For example, combining herbs with complementary actions can provide a more comprehensive therapeutic effect, such as blending anti-inflammatory herbs to manage chronic pain.

- **Antagonistic Effects**: Some herbs may counteract each other's effects. For instance, combining a sedative herb with a stimulant could diminish the efficacy of both.

Herb-Medication Interactions:

- **Altered Efficacy**: Herbs can influence the metabolism of pharmaceutical drugs, either increasing or decreasing their effectiveness. For example, St. John's Wort can reduce the effectiveness of certain antidepressants and contraceptives.

- **Adverse Reactions**: Some herbs may increase the risk of side effects or adverse reactions when taken with medications. For instance, combining herbs with anticoagulant properties, like garlic, with blood thinners can enhance bleeding risk.

2. Dosage and Proportions

Correct Dosage:

- **Research Recommended Dosages**: Ensure that each herb is used within its recommended dosage range. Dosage recommendations can vary based on the form of the herb (e.g., tincture, tea, capsule).

- **Start with Low Doses**: Begin with lower doses of a new herbal blend and gradually increase as needed. This helps assess tolerance and minimize the risk of adverse effects.

Proportions:

- **Balanced Formulation**: Use appropriate proportions of each herb to achieve a balanced blend. Overusing one herb can overshadow the effects of others and lead to imbalances.

- **Consult Herbal Literature**: Refer to established herbal texts or consult with an experienced herbalist for guidance on creating effective and safe herb combinations.

3. Preparation Methods

Appropriate Methods:

- **Correct Preparation**: Ensure herbs are prepared using methods suitable for their properties (e.g., tinctures for alcohol-soluble compounds, teas for water-soluble compounds).

- **Quality Control**: Use high-quality herbs from reputable sources to avoid contaminants and ensure potency.

Storage and Handling:

- **Proper Storage**: Store herbs and herbal blends in a cool, dry place away from light and moisture to maintain their efficacy.

- **Labeling**: Clearly label herbal preparations with ingredients, dosage instructions, and preparation dates to avoid confusion and ensure safe use.

4. Consider Individual Health Conditions

Pre-existing Conditions:

- **Assess Health Status**: Evaluate any pre-existing health conditions that may affect the safety or efficacy of herbal blends. For example, individuals with liver disease should use caution with herbs like echinacea that affect liver function.

- **Monitor Reactions**: Be vigilant for any unusual symptoms or adverse reactions when starting a new herbal blend, and discontinue use if negative effects occur.

Age and Sensitivity:

- **Age Considerations**: Adjust dosages and formulations based on age. Children, elderly individuals, and pregnant or breastfeeding women have different safety considerations and dosage requirements.

- **Allergies and Sensitivities**: Be aware of potential allergies or sensitivities to specific herbs. Perform a patch test or start with a small dose to identify any adverse reactions.

5. Consultation and Professional Guidance

Seek Professional Advice:

- **Consult Herbalists**: Work with a qualified herbalist or healthcare provider to develop personalized herbal blends and address specific health concerns. They can provide expertise on safe combinations and dosages.

- **Review with Healthcare Providers**: If you are on prescription medications or have a chronic health condition, consult your healthcare provider before starting any new herbal regimen. This helps to avoid potential interactions and ensure safe use.

Education and Resources:

- **Stay Informed**: Continuously educate yourself about herbal medicine through reputable sources, including books, research studies, and professional organizations.

- **Participate in Workshops**: Attend herbal medicine workshops or seminars to enhance your knowledge and skills in safely creating and using herbal blends.

6. Ethical and Environmental Considerations

Sustainable Sourcing:

- **Wildcrafting**: When foraging for herbs, follow ethical wildcrafting practices to avoid overharvesting and protect local ecosystems.

- **Organic and Sustainable**: Prefer herbs grown organically and sustainably to minimize exposure to pesticides and environmental contaminants.

Legal Regulations:

- **Compliance**: Be aware of local regulations regarding the use and sale of herbal products. Ensure that any herbal preparations comply with relevant legal requirements.

Creating balanced and effective herbal blends requires careful attention to safety and precaution. By understanding herb interactions, following appropriate dosage and preparation methods, considering individual health conditions, seeking professional guidance, and practicing ethical sourcing, you can maximize the benefits of herbal remedies while minimizing risks. Herbal medicine, when used responsibly and knowledgeably, can be a powerful tool for supporting health and well-being.

Simple Ingredients, Big Impact

Garlic: A Natural Antibiotic and Cholesterol Manager

Garlic (*Allium sativum*) has been revered for its medicinal properties for thousands of years. Known for its distinct flavor and aroma, garlic is also celebrated for its health benefits, including its natural antibiotic properties and its role in managing cholesterol levels. This section explores garlic's therapeutic effects, scientific evidence supporting its benefits, and practical ways to incorporate it into your diet.

1. Medicinal Properties of Garlic

Antibiotic Effects:

- **Active Compounds**: Garlic contains several sulfur-containing compounds, with allicin being the most studied. Allicin is formed when garlic is crushed or chopped and has demonstrated antimicrobial properties against a wide range of bacteria, fungi, and viruses.

- **Mechanism of Action**: Allicin disrupts bacterial cell membranes and inhibits the growth of microorganisms. It has shown efficacy against common pathogens such as *Staphylococcus aureus* and *Escherichia coli*.

- **Research Evidence**: Clinical studies have highlighted garlic's effectiveness in reducing the incidence of common infections, such as colds and flu. Some research indicates that garlic supplementation may also help in managing antibiotic-resistant infections.

Cholesterol Management:

- **Reduction of LDL Cholesterol**: Garlic has been shown to help lower low-density lipoprotein (LDL) cholesterol, often referred to as "bad" cholesterol. LDL cholesterol is a key contributor to atherosclerosis and cardiovascular disease.

- **Increase in HDL Cholesterol**: Some studies suggest that garlic may increase high-density lipoprotein (HDL) cholesterol, which is considered "good" cholesterol and helps protect against heart disease.

- **Mechanism of Action**: Garlic affects cholesterol levels by reducing the synthesis of cholesterol in the liver and promoting the excretion of cholesterol from the body. It may also enhance the antioxidant status, which helps protect lipids from oxidation.

2. Scientific Evidence Supporting Garlic's Benefits

Antibiotic Properties:

- **Studies on Antimicrobial Activity**: Research has demonstrated that garlic extracts can inhibit the growth of a variety of pathogens, including bacteria, fungi, and viruses. A review of clinical trials found that garlic can reduce the severity and duration of the common cold.

- **Effectiveness Against Antibiotic Resistance**: Some studies suggest that garlic may be effective against antibiotic-resistant bacteria, making it a valuable addition to conventional treatments for certain infections.

Cholesterol-Lowering Effects:

- **Meta-Analyses**: Several meta-analyses of clinical trials have confirmed that garlic supplementation can lead to a significant reduction in total cholesterol and LDL cholesterol levels. The extent of the reduction can vary based on the form and dose of garlic used.

- **Long-Term Benefits**: Long-term studies have shown that regular consumption of garlic can have beneficial effects on cardiovascular health, potentially reducing the risk of heart disease and stroke.

3. Incorporating Garlic into Your Diet

Fresh Garlic:

- **Preparation**: Crush or chop garlic and let it sit for a few minutes before cooking to maximize allicin formation. Raw garlic can be added to salads, dressings, or as a topping for various dishes.

- **Cooking**: Garlic can be sautéed, roasted, or added to recipes. However, cooking garlic at high temperatures for long periods can reduce its allicin content. For maximum benefit, consider incorporating both raw and cooked garlic into your meals.

Garlic Supplements:

- **Forms**: Garlic supplements are available in various forms, including capsules, tablets, and extracts. These supplements often contain standardized amounts of allicin or other active compounds.

- **Dosage**: The effective dosage of garlic supplements can vary. Studies often use doses ranging from 600 to 1,200 mg of garlic extract per day. It's important to follow the recommended dosage on the supplement label or consult a healthcare provider for personalized advice.

Garlic Oil:

- **Usage**: Garlic oil can be used in cooking or as a dietary supplement. It is typically made by infusing garlic in oil, and while it retains some of garlic's benefits, the allicin content may be lower compared to raw garlic.

4. Safety and Precautions

General Safety:

- **Allergies and Sensitivities**: Some individuals may experience gastrointestinal discomfort or allergic reactions to garlic. It's advisable to start with small amounts and monitor for any adverse effects.

- **Bleeding Risk**: Garlic has anticoagulant properties, which may increase the risk of bleeding, especially in individuals taking blood-thinning medications. Consult a healthcare provider if you are on such medications.

Drug Interactions:

- **Medications**: Garlic can interact with certain medications, including anticoagulants, antiplatelet drugs, and some HIV medications. If you are on medication or have a health condition, discuss garlic use with your healthcare provider.

Pregnancy and Breastfeeding:

- **Consultation**: Pregnant and breastfeeding women should consult their healthcare provider before using garlic supplements, as high doses may have effects on pregnancy or lactation.

5. Practical Applications and Recipes

Garlic-Infused Oil:

- **Recipe**: Infuse garlic in olive oil by heating crushed garlic in oil over low heat for 10-15 minutes. Strain and store in a clean, airtight container. Use as a flavorful addition to salads and dishes.

Garlic-Based Dressings:

- **Recipe**: Create a garlic vinaigrette by combining minced garlic with olive oil, lemon juice, Dijon mustard, and herbs. Use as a dressing for salads or a marinade for vegetables.

Garlic-Enhanced Soups and Stews:

- **Recipe**: Add minced or chopped garlic to soups and stews for added flavor and health benefits. Garlic pairs well with a variety of vegetables and meats.

Garlic is a powerful herb with proven benefits for antibiotic activity and cholesterol management. Its active compounds, especially allicin, contribute to its medicinal properties, offering a natural way to support immune health and cardiovascular well-being. Incorporating garlic into your diet, either through fresh cloves, supplements, or garlic-infused oil, can enhance your overall health while providing a flavorful addition to your meals. As with any supplement or dietary change, it's essential to consider individual health conditions and consult with healthcare professionals to ensure safe and effective use.

Cinnamon: Regulating Blood Sugar and Enhancing Circulation

Cinnamon (*Cinnamomum verum* or *Cinnamomum cassia*) is a popular spice known not only for its distinct flavor but also for its health benefits. Among its notable effects are its ability to help regulate blood sugar levels and enhance circulation. This section explores the medicinal properties of cinnamon, the scientific evidence supporting its benefits, and practical ways to incorporate it into your diet.

1. Medicinal Properties of Cinnamon

Blood Sugar Regulation:

- **Active Compounds**: Cinnamon contains bioactive compounds such as cinnamaldehyde, cinnamic acid, and various polyphenols. These compounds are believed to contribute to its ability to regulate blood sugar levels.

- **Mechanism of Action**: Cinnamon may improve insulin sensitivity, which helps the body use glucose more effectively. It can also slow the digestion of carbohydrates in the intestines, leading to a slower rise in blood sugar levels after meals.

- **Research Evidence**: Numerous studies have demonstrated cinnamon's potential benefits in managing blood sugar levels. For example, some research indicates that cinnamon supplementation can lower fasting blood glucose levels and improve hemoglobin A1c (a marker of long-term blood sugar control).

Circulatory Benefits:

- **Improved Blood Flow**: Cinnamon may enhance circulation by promoting vasodilation (the widening of blood vessels), which can improve blood flow and reduce blood pressure.

- **Antioxidant and Anti-Inflammatory Properties**: The antioxidants in cinnamon help reduce oxidative stress and inflammation, which can contribute to better cardiovascular health. These effects may indirectly support circulation and overall heart health.

- **Research Evidence**: Studies have shown that cinnamon consumption can have beneficial effects on blood pressure and cholesterol levels, which are important factors in maintaining good circulation and cardiovascular health.

2. Scientific Evidence Supporting Cinnamon's Benefits

Blood Sugar Regulation:

- **Clinical Trials**: Several clinical trials have found that cinnamon supplementation can lead to significant reductions in fasting blood glucose levels and improvements in insulin sensitivity. For instance, a meta-analysis of randomized controlled trials concluded that cinnamon had a modest but statistically significant effect on lowering blood glucose and improving insulin sensitivity.

- **Dosage and Form**: Effective dosages in studies typically range from 1 to 6 grams of cinnamon per day. Cinnamon can be consumed in various forms, including powdered spice, capsules, or extracts.

Circulatory Benefits:

- **Blood Pressure and Lipid Levels**: Research has shown that cinnamon may have a beneficial impact on blood pressure and lipid profiles. A study published in the *Journal of Clinical Nutrition* found that cinnamon supplementation led to reductions in both systolic and diastolic blood pressure in individuals with type 2 diabetes.

- **Antioxidant Activity**: Cinnamon's high antioxidant content helps combat oxidative stress, which is linked to cardiovascular disease. Studies have demonstrated that cinnamon can increase antioxidant levels and reduce markers of inflammation.

3. Incorporating Cinnamon into Your Diet

Culinary Uses:

- **Spice Blends**: Add ground cinnamon to spice blends for savory dishes. It complements meats, stews, and curries, adding warmth and depth of flavor.

- **Baked Goods**: Incorporate cinnamon into baked goods such as muffins, bread, and cookies. It pairs well with fruits, nuts, and other spices.
- **Beverages**: Sprinkle cinnamon on coffee, tea, or hot chocolate. You can also add it to smoothies for a flavorful and health-boosting kick.

Supplement Forms:

- **Capsules and Tablets**: Cinnamon supplements are available in various forms, including capsules and tablets. These often contain concentrated cinnamon extract, which provides a standardized dose of active compounds.
- **Cinnamon Extract**: Liquid extracts of cinnamon can be used in small amounts as a dietary supplement. Follow dosage instructions on the label or consult a healthcare provider for personalized advice.

Recipes:

- **Cinnamon-Infused Water**: Add a cinnamon stick to a jug of water and let it infuse overnight. This can be a refreshing and healthful beverage option.
- **Cinnamon Oatmeal**: Stir ground cinnamon into your morning oatmeal or yogurt for added flavor and health benefits.

4. Safety and Precautions

Types of Cinnamon:

- **Ceylon Cinnamon**: Often referred to as "true cinnamon," Ceylon cinnamon is considered safer for regular consumption due to its lower coumarin content. Coumarin is a compound that can be harmful in large amounts.
- **Cassia Cinnamon**: Commonly used in food products, Cassia cinnamon contains higher levels of coumarin. While occasional use is generally safe, excessive intake should be avoided.

Drug Interactions:

- **Blood Sugar Medications**: Cinnamon may enhance the effects of blood sugar-lowering medications, potentially leading to hypoglycemia (low blood sugar). Monitor blood sugar levels and consult a healthcare provider if you are on medication for diabetes.

Allergies and Sensitivities:

- **Allergic Reactions**: While rare, some individuals may experience allergic reactions to cinnamon. Symptoms can include skin rashes or digestive discomfort. If you suspect an allergy, discontinue use and seek medical advice.

Pregnancy and Breastfeeding:

- **Consultation**: Pregnant and breastfeeding women should consult their healthcare provider before using cinnamon supplements, particularly in high doses.

5. Practical Applications and Recipes

Cinnamon Tea:

- **Recipe**: Boil water and steep a cinnamon stick for 10 minutes. Optionally, add honey or lemon for additional flavor.

Cinnamon Smoothie:

- **Recipe**: Blend 1 teaspoon of ground cinnamon with banana, yogurt, and a handful of berries for a nutritious smoothie.

Cinnamon-Seasoned Nuts:

- **Recipe**: Toss almonds or walnuts with a sprinkle of cinnamon and a touch of honey, then roast in the oven for a healthy snack.

Cinnamon is more than just a flavorful spice; it offers significant health benefits, particularly in regulating blood sugar levels and enhancing circulation. Its active compounds provide antioxidant, anti-inflammatory, and insulin-sensitizing effects that contribute to overall well-being. By incorporating cinnamon into your diet in various forms and enjoying its culinary versatility, you can take advantage of its therapeutic properties while adding a delightful flavor to your meals. As always, consider individual health conditions and consult with a healthcare provider before making significant changes to your diet or supplement regimen.

Turmeric: Anti-Inflammatory Powerhouse

Turmeric (*Curcuma longa*) is a vibrant yellow spice derived from the rhizome of the turmeric plant. It has been used for thousands of years in traditional medicine, particularly in Ayurveda and Traditional Chinese Medicine, due to its potent anti-inflammatory and antioxidant properties. This section delves into turmeric's benefits, the science behind its effects, and practical ways to incorporate it into your diet.

1. Medicinal Properties of Turmeric

Anti-Inflammatory Effects:

- **Active Compounds**: The primary active compound in turmeric is curcumin. Curcumin is a polyphenol with strong anti-inflammatory properties. It works by inhibiting various inflammatory pathways, including the inhibition of nuclear factor-kappa B (NF-kB), a transcription factor involved in inflammation.

- **Mechanism of Action**: Curcumin modulates the activity of inflammatory cytokines and enzymes such as cyclooxygenase-2 (COX-2) and lipoxygenase. By reducing the expression of these inflammatory mediators, curcumin helps mitigate inflammation in the body.

- **Research Evidence**: Numerous studies have demonstrated curcumin's effectiveness in reducing inflammation and providing relief from conditions characterized by chronic inflammation, such as arthritis, inflammatory bowel disease, and cardiovascular disease.

Antioxidant Properties:

- **Free Radical Scavenging**: Curcumin also has significant antioxidant properties. It neutralizes free radicals and boosts the body's own antioxidant enzymes, such as superoxide dismutase and catalase.

- **Oxidative Stress Reduction**: By reducing oxidative stress, curcumin helps prevent damage to cells and tissues, which is linked to aging and various chronic diseases.

2. Scientific Evidence Supporting Turmeric's Benefits

Anti-Inflammatory Effects:

- **Clinical Trials**: Several clinical trials have shown that curcumin can significantly reduce markers of inflammation, such as C-reactive protein (CRP) and interleukin-6 (IL-6). For example, studies on patients with osteoarthritis have reported improvements in pain and function with curcumin supplementation.

- **Chronic Disease Management**: Research suggests that curcumin may be beneficial in managing chronic inflammatory diseases, including rheumatoid arthritis, inflammatory bowel disease, and metabolic syndrome.

Antioxidant Effects:

- **Studies on Oxidative Stress**: Clinical studies have demonstrated that curcumin can increase antioxidant levels and decrease oxidative stress markers. This effect is beneficial for overall health and may help in reducing the risk of chronic diseases related to oxidative damage.

3. Incorporating Turmeric into Your Diet

Culinary Uses:

- **Spice Blends**: Turmeric is a key ingredient in many spice blends, such as curry powder. It adds flavor and color to dishes like curries, stews, and soups.

- **Golden Milk**: This traditional beverage combines turmeric with milk (or dairy-free alternatives) and often includes additional spices like black pepper and ginger. Golden milk is known for its soothing and anti-inflammatory properties.

- **Smoothies and Juices**: Add a teaspoon of turmeric powder to your smoothies or fresh juices for an extra health boost.

Supplement Forms:

- **Capsules and Tablets**: Turmeric supplements are available in various forms, including capsules and tablets. These often contain standardized curcumin extracts with higher concentrations of active compounds.

- **Curcumin Extracts**: Extracts of curcumin, often combined with black pepper (which enhances absorption), can be a potent way to increase intake and benefit from turmeric's anti-inflammatory effects.

Recipes:

- **Turmeric Rice**: Add a teaspoon of turmeric to your rice while cooking for a colorful and flavorful dish. It pairs well with a variety of proteins and vegetables.

- **Turmeric Tea**: Boil water with a teaspoon of turmeric powder, a slice of ginger, and a dash of black pepper. Strain and enjoy as a soothing and healthful tea.

4. Safety and Precautions

Dosage:

- **Recommended Dosages**: Turmeric and curcumin supplements are generally safe when taken within recommended dosages. Typical dosages range from 500 to 2,000 mg of curcumin per day. It's important to follow the dosage instructions on supplement labels or consult a healthcare provider.

Possible Side Effects:

- **Gastrointestinal Issues**: High doses of turmeric can cause gastrointestinal discomfort, including nausea, diarrhea, and stomach cramps. Starting with a lower dose and gradually increasing it can help mitigate these effects.

- **Allergic Reactions**: Although rare, some individuals may experience allergic reactions to turmeric. Symptoms can include skin rashes or itching. Discontinue use if an allergic reaction occurs.

Drug Interactions:

- **Blood Thinners**: Turmeric may enhance the effects of anticoagulant and antiplatelet medications, increasing the risk of bleeding. If you are on such medications, consult your healthcare provider before using turmeric supplements.

- **Gastrointestinal Medications**: Turmeric may affect the absorption of certain medications or interact with medications used for gastrointestinal conditions. Consult a healthcare provider if you have concerns.

Pregnancy and Breastfeeding:

- **Consultation**: Pregnant and breastfeeding women should consult their healthcare provider before using high doses of turmeric supplements, as excessive amounts may have adverse effects.

5. Practical Applications and Recipes

Turmeric-Infused Oil:

- **Recipe**: Infuse olive oil with turmeric by heating it with turmeric powder over low heat for 10-15 minutes. Strain and use as a flavorful addition to dressings and marinades.

Turmeric and Ginger Tea:

- **Recipe**: Combine fresh turmeric root, ginger, and honey in hot water. Steep for 10 minutes, then strain and enjoy a soothing tea.

Turmeric-Seasoned Vegetables:

- **Recipe**: Toss vegetables with olive oil, turmeric, cumin, and a pinch of salt. Roast in the oven for a delicious and healthful side dish.

Turmeric is a remarkable spice with powerful anti-inflammatory and antioxidant properties, thanks primarily to its active compound, curcumin. Its potential benefits in managing inflammation and oxidative stress make it a valuable addition to both culinary and therapeutic applications. By incorporating turmeric into your diet through various forms and recipes, you can harness its health benefits while adding flavor and color to your meals. As with any supplement or dietary change, consider individual health conditions and consult with a healthcare provider for personalized advice.

Ginger: Digestive Aid and Immune Booster

Ginger (*Zingiber officinale*) is a widely used spice with a long history of medicinal use, particularly in traditional medicine systems such as Ayurveda and Traditional Chinese Medicine. Renowned for its distinct flavor and versatility, ginger is celebrated for its health benefits, particularly its ability to aid digestion and boost the immune system. This section explores ginger's therapeutic effects, the scientific evidence supporting its benefits, and practical ways to incorporate it into your diet.

1. Medicinal Properties of Ginger

Digestive Aid:

- **Active Compounds**: Ginger contains several bioactive compounds, including gingerol, shogaol, and paradol. These compounds contribute to its digestive benefits.

- **Mechanism of Action**: Ginger aids digestion by stimulating the production of digestive enzymes and increasing gastric motility, which helps to move food through the digestive tract. It also has antiemetic properties, which help reduce nausea and vomiting.

- **Research Evidence**: Studies have shown that ginger can be effective in alleviating symptoms of nausea, including morning sickness during pregnancy, nausea induced by chemotherapy, and motion sickness. Additionally, ginger can help with indigestion by reducing bloating and discomfort.

Immune System Support:

- **Anti-Inflammatory Effects**: Ginger's anti-inflammatory properties, attributed mainly to its gingerol content, help reduce inflammation and support immune function. Inflammation can compromise immune response, so reducing it can aid overall immune health.

- **Antioxidant Properties**: Ginger has potent antioxidant effects that help protect cells from oxidative stress and damage, which is beneficial for maintaining a robust immune system.

- **Research Evidence**: Clinical studies suggest that ginger can enhance immune function by increasing the production of certain immune cells and improving the body's ability to fight infections. It has also been shown to reduce the duration and severity of colds and flu.

2. Scientific Evidence Supporting Ginger's Benefits

Digestive Aid:

- **Clinical Trials**: Research has consistently demonstrated ginger's effectiveness in managing nausea and vomiting. For example, a study published in the *Journal of Clinical Oncology* found that ginger was effective in reducing chemotherapy induced nausea.

- **Digestive Health**: Studies have shown that ginger can help alleviate symptoms of indigestion and bloating. A review published in *The Journal of Gastroenterology* highlighted ginger's role in improving digestion and reducing gastrointestinal discomfort.

Immune System Support:

- **Immunomodulatory Effects**: Research has indicated that ginger can positively affect the immune system by modulating inflammatory responses and enhancing immune cell activity. For instance, a study in *Phytotherapy Research* found that ginger extract improved immune responses in individuals with respiratory infections.

- **Cold and Flu Relief**: Clinical trials have shown that ginger can reduce the severity and duration of cold and flu symptoms. Its antioxidant and anti-inflammatory properties contribute to its ability to support the immune system.

3. Incorporating Ginger into Your Diet

Culinary Uses:

- **Fresh Ginger**: Use fresh ginger root in cooking by grating or chopping it. It adds a zesty flavor to stir-fries, soups, and marinades. Fresh ginger can also be steeped to make ginger tea.

- **Ground Ginger**: Ground ginger is a common ingredient in baking and spice blends. It can be added to cookies, cakes, and savory dishes for a warm, spicy flavor.

- **Ginger Juice**: Fresh ginger can be juiced and added to smoothies or beverages. It pairs well with citrus fruits and other health-boosting ingredients.

Supplement Forms:

- **Ginger Capsules**: Ginger supplements are available in capsule form and are often used for therapeutic purposes. These capsules typically contain concentrated ginger extract.

- **Ginger Extracts**: Liquid ginger extracts can be used in small amounts as a dietary supplement or added to water or tea for an extra boost.

Recipes:

- **Ginger Tea**: Slice fresh ginger and steep it in hot water for 10 minutes. Add honey and lemon for additional flavor and health benefits.

- **Ginger-Lemonade**: Blend fresh ginger with lemon juice, water, and a touch of honey for a refreshing and immune-boosting drink.

- **Ginger Stir-Fry**: Incorporate sliced or minced ginger into vegetable or meat stir-fries for added flavor and digestive support.

4. Safety and Precautions

Dosage:

- **Recommended Dosages**: Ginger is generally safe for most people when consumed in moderate amounts as part of a meal. For therapeutic purposes, typical dosages range from 1 to 3 grams of ginger per day. Ginger supplements should be taken according to the manufacturer's instructions or a healthcare provider's advice.

Possible Side Effects:

- **Gastrointestinal Issues**: High doses of ginger may cause gastrointestinal discomfort, such as heartburn, diarrhea, or stomach upset. Starting with a lower dose and gradually increasing it can help mitigate these effects.

- **Allergic Reactions**: Although rare, some individuals may experience allergic reactions to ginger. Symptoms can include rash, itching, or swelling. Discontinue use if an allergic reaction occurs.

Drug Interactions:

- **Blood Thinners**: Ginger may have anticoagulant effects and can enhance the effects of blood-thinning medications, increasing the risk of bleeding. If you are on anticoagulants or antiplatelet drugs, consult a healthcare provider before using ginger supplements.

- **Diabetes Medications**: Ginger may lower blood sugar levels, so if you are on diabetes medication, monitor your blood sugar levels and consult your healthcare provider.

Pregnancy and Breastfeeding:

- **Consultation**: Ginger is generally considered safe during pregnancy and breastfeeding when consumed in moderate amounts. However, high doses should be avoided, and pregnant or breastfeeding women should consult a healthcare provider before using ginger supplements.

5. Practical Applications and Recipes

Ginger-Infused Honey:

- **Recipe**: Infuse honey with fresh ginger slices by heating them together in a jar. Use as a natural remedy for sore throats or add to tea.

Ginger and Turmeric Tea:

- **Recipe**: Combine fresh ginger root and turmeric in boiling water. Steep for 10 minutes, strain, and enjoy a warming and healthful beverage.

Ginger-Seasoned Roasted Vegetables:

- **Recipe**: Toss vegetables with olive oil, ginger, garlic, and your favorite herbs. Roast until tender for a flavorful and digestive-friendly side dish.

Ginger is a versatile and powerful spice with significant health benefits, particularly in aiding digestion and boosting the immune system. Its active compounds, especially gingerol, provide anti-inflammatory and antioxidant effects that contribute to overall well-being. Incorporating ginger into your diet, whether through fresh root, ground spice, or supplements, can enhance your digestive health and support your immune function. As always, consider individual health conditions and consult with a healthcare provider for personalized advice on using ginger for therapeutic purposes.

Honey: Healing Wounds and Soothing Sore Throats

Honey is a natural substance produced by bees from the nectar of flowers. It has been used for centuries not only as a sweetener but also for its medicinal properties. Known for its antimicrobial and soothing qualities, honey is particularly effective in wound healing and alleviating sore throats. This section explores honey's therapeutic benefits, the scientific evidence supporting its uses, and practical ways to incorporate it into your wellness routine.

1. Medicinal Properties of Honey

Wound Healing:

- **Antimicrobial Properties**: Honey has natural antimicrobial properties due to its low pH, high sugar content, and the presence of hydrogen peroxide and other bioactive compounds. These factors create an environment that inhibits the growth of bacteria and promotes wound healing.

- **Anti-Inflammatory Effects**: Honey can reduce inflammation in wounds and skin irritations. Its soothing properties help to calm the affected area and accelerate the healing process.

- **Research Evidence**: Numerous studies have demonstrated honey's effectiveness in treating wounds, including burns, cuts, and ulcers. For instance, honey has been shown to promote faster healing and reduce infection rates in wound care settings. Medical-grade honey, such as Manuka honey, is often used in clinical settings for its enhanced antimicrobial properties.

Soothing Sore Throats:

- **Coating and Soothing**: Honey forms a protective coating in the throat, which helps to soothe irritation and reduce coughing. Its viscous texture helps to trap and remove irritants from the throat lining.

- **Antimicrobial and Anti-Inflammatory Properties**: Honey's antimicrobial and anti-inflammatory effects help to reduce the severity and duration of sore throats. It can help alleviate symptoms associated with throat infections and irritations.

- **Research Evidence**: Studies have shown that honey can be effective in relieving symptoms of sore throats and coughs. For example, research published in the *Journal of Alternative and Complementary Medicine* found that honey was as effective as cough medicine in reducing the frequency and severity of coughs in children.

2. Scientific Evidence Supporting Honey's Benefits

Wound Healing:

- **Clinical Trials**: Clinical studies have demonstrated that honey, especially Manuka honey, can significantly speed up wound healing and reduce infection rates. For example, a study published in *The Cochrane Database of Systematic Reviews* found that honey was effective in treating diabetic foot ulcers and other chronic wounds.

- **Mechanism of Action**: Honey's high sugar concentration creates a hypertonic environment that draws moisture out of bacteria and prevents their growth. The production of hydrogen peroxide further contributes to its antimicrobial effect.

Soothing Sore Throats:

- **Studies on Cough and Throat Irritation**: Research has shown that honey can be as effective as traditional cough medicines in reducing cough frequency and severity. A study published in *Pediatrics* found that honey was more effective than a placebo in reducing nighttime coughing and improving sleep in children with upper respiratory infections.

- **Traditional Use**: Honey has long been used in traditional medicine for soothing sore throats and coughs. Its use is supported by both historical practices and modern research.

3. Incorporating Honey into Your Routine

Culinary Uses:

- **Sweetener**: Use honey as a natural sweetener in tea, coffee, or other beverages. It can also be added to yogurt, oatmeal, or smoothies for a touch of sweetness and added health benefits.

- **Cooking and Baking**: Incorporate honey into recipes for baked goods, marinades, dressings, and sauces. It adds a unique flavor and nutritional value to dishes.

Medicinal Uses:

- **Sore Throat Relief**: Take a spoonful of honey on its own or mix it with warm water and lemon juice to soothe a sore throat. Honey can also be added to herbal teas for additional soothing effects.

- **Wound Care**: For minor wounds or burns, apply a thin layer of honey directly to the affected area and cover with a clean bandage. Change the dressing and reapply honey as needed.

Recipes:

- **Honey Lemon Tea**: Mix 1-2 tablespoons of honey with the juice of half a lemon in hot water. This soothing drink can help alleviate sore throats and provide a comforting remedy.

- **Honey-Infused Glaze**: Create a honey glaze by combining honey with mustard or soy sauce. Use it to add flavor to roasted vegetables, meats, or tofu.

4. Safety and Precautions

Infant Safety:

- **Botulism Risk**: Honey should not be given to infants under 1 year of age due to the risk of botulism, a rare but serious illness caused by bacteria that can be present in honey.

Allergic Reactions:

- **Potential Allergies**: Some individuals may have allergic reactions to honey, particularly if they are allergic to pollen or bee products. Symptoms can include itching, swelling, or hives. Discontinue use and seek medical advice if an allergic reaction occurs.

Diabetes and Blood Sugar:

- **Sugar Content**: Honey is high in natural sugars and can affect blood sugar levels. Individuals with diabetes or those managing blood sugar levels should monitor their intake and consult with a healthcare provider.

Quality of Honey:

- **Choosing Honey**: Opt for raw, unprocessed honey whenever possible to ensure maximum health benefits. Processed honey may lose some of its beneficial properties during refining.

5. Practical Applications and Recipes

Honey Face Mask:

- **Recipe**: Apply a thin layer of honey to the face and leave it on for 15-20 minutes before rinsing off. Honey's moisturizing and antibacterial properties can help with acne and skin hydration.

Honey and Ginger Tonic:

- **Recipe**: Mix 1 tablespoon of honey with freshly grated ginger and a splash of lemon juice. This tonic can help soothe a sore throat and provide a natural immune boost.

Honey and Cinnamon Remedy:

- **Recipe**: Combine honey with a pinch of cinnamon and take it daily to support digestive health and boost the immune system.

Honey is a versatile natural remedy with well-documented benefits for wound healing and soothing sore throats. Its antimicrobial, anti-inflammatory, and soothing properties make it a valuable addition to both your kitchen and first-aid kit. By incorporating honey into your daily routine and using it wisely, you can take advantage of its therapeutic effects while enjoying its natural sweetness. Always consider individual health conditions and consult with a healthcare provider for personalized advice on using honey for medicinal purposes.

Apple Cider Vinegar: Detoxification and Weight Management

Apple cider vinegar (ACV) is a popular fermented liquid made from apple juice and a culture of yeast and bacteria. It has been used for centuries in traditional medicine and cooking. Its purported benefits include detoxification, weight management, and overall health improvement. This section explores the benefits of apple cider vinegar, the science behind its effects, and practical ways to incorporate it into your lifestyle.

1. Medicinal Properties of Apple Cider Vinegar

Detoxification:

- **Acetic Acid**: The main active component of ACV is acetic acid, which is believed to play a role in detoxification. Acetic acid helps promote the body's natural detoxification processes by enhancing digestion and supporting liver function.

- **Supporting Digestive Health**: ACV can aid digestion by increasing stomach acid production, which helps break down food more efficiently and improves nutrient absorption. This can contribute to a more effective detoxification process.

- **Research Evidence**: Some studies suggest that ACV can support detoxification by enhancing metabolic processes and promoting the elimination of toxins through urine. However, more research is needed to fully understand its impact on detoxification.

Weight Management:

- **Appetite Control**: ACV has been shown to have appetite-suppressing effects, which can help with weight management. It is thought to increase feelings of fullness and reduce overall calorie intake.

- **Blood Sugar Regulation**: ACV can help stabilize blood sugar levels, which is important for weight management. By improving insulin sensitivity and lowering postprandial glucose levels, ACV can support weight loss efforts.

- **Research Evidence**: Several studies have demonstrated that ACV can assist with weight loss. For example, a study published in *Bioscience, Biotechnology, and Biochemistry* found that participants who consumed ACV daily lost more weight compared to those who did not. ACV was also shown to reduce body fat percentage and waist circumference.

2. Scientific Evidence Supporting ACV's Benefits

Detoxification:

- **Studies on Metabolic Health**: Research has suggested that ACV can enhance metabolic health by promoting the breakdown of fats and reducing inflammation. For instance, a study published in *The American Journal of Clinical Nutrition* found that acetic acid supplementation improved metabolic markers in overweight individuals.

- **Liver Health**: Some animal studies have indicated that ACV may support liver function by reducing oxidative stress and promoting the detoxification process. However, human studies are needed to confirm these effects.

Weight Management:

- **Clinical Trials**: Clinical trials have shown that ACV can aid in weight management. In a study published in *The Journal of Functional Foods*, participants who consumed ACV daily experienced significant reductions in body weight and body fat.

- **Mechanisms of Action**: ACV's impact on appetite regulation and blood sugar levels is supported by evidence showing that it can enhance satiety and improve insulin sensitivity. Research published in *Appetite* found that ACV consumption led to reduced calorie intake and improved satiety in overweight individuals.

3. Incorporating Apple Cider Vinegar into Your Routine

Culinary Uses:

- **Salad Dressings**: Use ACV as a tangy component in salad dressings. Combine it with olive oil, mustard, and herbs for a healthy and flavorful dressing.

- **Marinades**: ACV can be used in marinades for meats and vegetables, adding a zesty flavor while promoting digestion.

Detoxification and Weight Management:

- **ACV Drink**: Mix 1-2 tablespoons of ACV with a glass of water and a teaspoon of honey (optional). Drink this mixture before meals to support digestion and potentially aid in weight management.

- **ACV Shots**: For a more concentrated dose, take a shot of diluted ACV. However, be cautious with this method as ACV is highly acidic and may irritate the digestive tract.

Recipes:

- **Apple Cider Vinegar Tea**: Steep a tea bag in hot water and add 1-2 tablespoons of ACV and a squeeze of lemon juice. This combination can be a soothing and healthful beverage.

- **ACV Smoothie**: Add a tablespoon of ACV to your morning smoothie for an extra health boost. It pairs well with fruits and greens.

4. Safety and Precautions

Dosage:

- **Recommended Dosages**: For most people, consuming 1-2 tablespoons of ACV per day, diluted in water, is considered safe. Start with a smaller amount to assess tolerance and gradually increase if needed.

Possible Side Effects:

- **Digestive Irritation**: ACV is highly acidic and may cause digestive discomfort, such as heartburn or irritation in the esophagus. Dilute ACV in water to reduce its acidity and avoid consuming it on an empty stomach.

- **Tooth Enamel Erosion**: The acidity of ACV can erode tooth enamel over time. To minimize this risk, drink ACV through a straw and rinse your mouth with water after consumption.

Drug Interactions:

- **Diabetes Medications**: ACV may lower blood sugar levels, which can interact with diabetes medications. Monitor blood sugar levels closely and consult with a healthcare provider if you are on diabetes medication.

- **Diuretics and Laxatives**: ACV may have diuretic effects and could interact with medications that affect fluid balance. Consult with a healthcare provider if you are using diuretics or laxatives.

Pregnancy and Breastfeeding:

- **Consultation**: Pregnant and breastfeeding women should consult a healthcare provider before using ACV supplements or consuming large amounts of ACV, as safety during pregnancy and lactation has not been extensively studied.

5. Practical Applications and Recipes

ACV Detox Bath:

- **Recipe**: Add 1-2 cups of ACV to a warm bath and soak for 20-30 minutes. The detox bath can help with relaxation and may support the body's natural detoxification processes.

Honey and ACV Tonic:

- **Recipe**: Mix 1 tablespoon of ACV with 1 tablespoon of honey in a glass of warm water. This tonic can be a soothing drink that combines the benefits of both ACV and honey.

ACV-Infused Smoothie:

- **Recipe**: Blend a tablespoon of ACV with spinach, apple, banana, and a splash of water. This smoothie can be a nutritious addition to your diet with the benefits of ACV.

Apple cider vinegar is a versatile natural remedy with potential benefits for detoxification and weight management. Its acetic acid content contributes to improved digestion, appetite control, and blood sugar regulation. By incorporating ACV into your diet and routine, you can leverage its health benefits while enjoying its tangy flavor. As with any supplement or dietary change, consider individual health conditions and consult with a healthcare provider for personalized advice on using apple cider vinegar effectively.

Lemon: Vitamin C Source and Alkalizing Agent

Lemon (*Citrus limon*) is a widely recognized fruit known for its tangy flavor and numerous health benefits. Rich in vitamin C and other beneficial compounds, lemon plays a significant role in supporting immune function, promoting detoxification, and maintaining overall health. This section explores the health benefits of lemon, the science behind its effects, and practical ways to incorporate it into your daily routine.

1. Medicinal Properties of Lemon

Vitamin C Source:

- **High Vitamin C Content**: Lemons are an excellent source of vitamin C (ascorbic acid), a powerful antioxidant that is essential for maintaining a healthy immune system and overall cellular health.

- **Immune Support**: Vitamin C is crucial for the synthesis of collagen, a protein that supports skin, blood vessels, and connective tissues. It also enhances the immune response by stimulating the production of white blood cells and improving their function.

- **Research Evidence**: Numerous studies have demonstrated the benefits of vitamin C in reducing the severity and duration of common colds and enhancing overall immune function. For example, research published in *Nutrients* has shown that adequate vitamin C intake can reduce the risk of infections and support recovery.

Alkalizing Agent:

- **Acid-Alkaline Balance**: Despite their acidic taste, lemons have an alkalizing effect on the body once metabolized. They help balance the body's pH levels, which can support overall health and reduce the risk of chronic diseases associated with an acidic environment.

- **Detoxification**: The alkalizing effect of lemons supports the body's natural detoxification processes by promoting the elimination of toxins and waste products. This can enhance liver function and overall well-being.

- **Research Evidence**: Although lemons are acidic in nature, their consumption has been associated with increased alkalinity in the body. A study published in *The Journal of Clinical Biochemistry and Nutrition* found that lemon juice could positively affect urinary pH levels, contributing to a more alkaline environment.

2. Scientific Evidence Supporting Lemon's Benefits

Vitamin C:

- **Immune System**: Vitamin C's role in immune support is well-documented. Clinical studies, such as those published in *The Cochrane Database of Systematic Reviews*, have shown that vitamin C supplementation can reduce the duration and severity of colds.

- **Antioxidant Effects**: Vitamin C is a potent antioxidant that helps protect cells from oxidative stress. Research published in *The Journal of Nutrition* highlights the role of vitamin C in reducing inflammation and supporting cardiovascular health.

Alkalizing Effect:

- **Acid-Base Balance**: Research supports the concept that lemon juice, despite its acidic nature, can have an alkalizing effect on the body. Studies have shown that lemon juice can help maintain a balanced pH level in the body and support overall health.

- **Detoxification**: Lemon's role in detoxification has been explored in studies that highlight its ability to enhance liver function and support the elimination of waste products.

3. Incorporating Lemon into Your Routine

Culinary Uses:

- **Lemon Juice**: Squeeze fresh lemon juice into water, tea, or salads for a refreshing and healthful addition. Lemon juice can also be used in marinades, dressings, and sauces to enhance flavor and nutritional value.
- **Lemon Zest**: Use lemon zest (the outer peel) to add a burst of flavor to baked goods, savory dishes, and beverages. Lemon zest contains essential oils and nutrients that contribute to its health benefits.

Detoxification and Health:

- **Lemon Water**: Start your day with a glass of warm lemon water. This simple routine can aid digestion, support detoxification, and provide a boost of vitamin C.
- **Lemon Tea**: Add lemon slices to herbal tea for an added health boost and a pleasant flavor. Lemon tea can support digestion and provide a soothing drink.

Recipes:

- **Lemonade**: Make a refreshing lemonade by mixing freshly squeezed lemon juice with water and a natural sweetener like honey or stevia. This drink can be a hydrating and immune-supporting beverage.
- **Lemon-Infused Water**: Add lemon slices to a pitcher of water and refrigerate. This can encourage increased water consumption and provide a subtle citrus flavor.

4. Safety and Precautions

Tooth Enamel:

- **Acidic Nature**: Lemon juice is highly acidic and can erode tooth enamel over time. To protect your teeth, drink lemon water through a straw and rinse your mouth with water after consuming lemon juice.

Gastrointestinal Issues:

- **Acid Sensitivity**: Individuals with acid reflux or sensitive stomachs may experience discomfort from acidic foods and beverages. If you have these conditions, consume lemon in moderation and consult with a healthcare provider.

Allergies:

- **Possible Allergic Reactions**: Although rare, some individuals may have allergic reactions to citrus fruits. Symptoms can include itching, swelling, or rash. Discontinue use if an allergic reaction occurs.

5. Practical Applications and Recipes

Lemon and Ginger Detox Drink:

- **Recipe**: Combine lemon juice with freshly grated ginger and warm water. This detox drink supports digestion, boosts immunity, and provides a refreshing start to your day.

Lemon and Honey Facial Toner:

- **Recipe**: Mix lemon juice with honey and apply it to your face as a natural toner. This combination can help with acne and skin hydration.

Lemon Herb Marinade:

- **Recipe**: Create a marinade by mixing lemon juice with olive oil, garlic, and herbs. Use it to marinate chicken, fish, or vegetables for a flavorful and healthful dish.

Conclusion

Lemon is a versatile fruit with significant health benefits, including its high vitamin C content and alkalizing effects. Its role in supporting immune function, promoting detoxification, and maintaining acid-base balance makes it a valuable addition to a healthy lifestyle. By incorporating lemon into your diet and daily routine, you can enjoy its refreshing flavor while reaping its numerous health benefits. As with any dietary changes, consider individual health conditions and consult with a healthcare provider for personalized advice on using lemon effectively.

Detailed Recipes and Preparations for Each Ingredient

In this section, we'll delve into the preparation and use of each of the key natural ingredients highlighted in your book. We'll provide detailed recipes and methods for incorporating garlic, cinnamon, turmeric, ginger, honey, apple cider vinegar, and lemon into your daily routine to maximize their health benefits.

1. Garlic: A Natural Antibiotic and Cholesterol Manager

Garlic Infused Oil:

- **Ingredients**:
    - 1 cup olive oil
    - 4-5 cloves garlic, peeled and crushed
- **Instructions**:
1. Combine garlic and olive oil in a small saucepan.

2.   Heat over low heat for about 20 minutes, making sure the garlic does not burn.

3.   Allow the mixture to cool, then strain out the garlic.

4.   Store the garlic-infused oil in a clean, airtight bottle in the refrigerator for up to 2 weeks.

- **Usage**: Use this oil for cooking or as a flavorful addition to salads and pasta dishes.

Garlic and Lemon Detox Drink:

- **Ingredients**:
    - 2 cloves garlic, minced
    - Juice of 1 lemon
    - 1 cup warm water
    - Honey to taste (optional)

- **Instructions**:

1.   Combine minced garlic and lemon juice in warm water.

2.   Stir well and let it sit for 10 minutes.

3.   Strain the garlic out if desired.

4.   Add honey if using and drink immediately.

- **Usage**: Drink this detox beverage in the morning to support immune function and digestion.

2. Cinnamon: Regulating Blood Sugar and Enhancing Circulation

Cinnamon Tea:

- **Ingredients**:
    - 1 cinnamon stick or 1 teaspoon ground cinnamon
    - 1 cup hot water
    - Honey or lemon to taste (optional)

- **Instructions**:

1.   Place the cinnamon stick or ground cinnamon in a cup.

2.   Pour hot water over it and let it steep for 5-10 minutes.

3.   Remove the cinnamon stick or strain out the ground cinnamon.

4.   Add honey or lemon if desired.

- **Usage**: Drink cinnamon tea in the morning or before meals to help regulate blood sugar levels and enhance circulation.

Cinnamon-Spiced Oatmeal:

- **Ingredients**:
    - 1 cup rolled oats
    - 2 cups water or milk
    - 1 teaspoon ground cinnamon
    - 1 tablespoon honey or maple syrup
    - Fresh fruit or nuts for topping (optional)

- **Instructions**:

1.   Combine oats and water or milk in a pot.

2.   Bring to a boil, then reduce heat and simmer for 5-7 minutes.

3.   Stir in ground cinnamon and sweetener.

4.   Top with fresh fruit or nuts if desired.

- **Usage**: Enjoy as a nutritious breakfast or snack to benefit from cinnamon's blood sugar-regulating properties.

3. Turmeric: Anti-Inflammatory Powerhouse

Golden Milk:

- **Ingredients**:
    - 1 cup milk (dairy or plant-based)
    - 1 teaspoon ground turmeric
    - 1/2 teaspoon ground black pepper
    - 1 tablespoon honey or maple syrup
    - 1/2 teaspoon ground cinnamon (optional)

- **Instructions**:

1. Heat the milk in a saucepan over medium heat.

2. Stir in turmeric, black pepper, and cinnamon if using.

3. Continue to heat until hot, but not boiling.

4. Remove from heat and stir in honey or maple syrup.

- **Usage**: Drink golden milk before bed or as a soothing beverage to reduce inflammation and support overall health.

Turmeric Paste:

- **Ingredients**:
    - 1/4 cup ground turmeric
    - 1/2 cup water
    - 1/4 teaspoon ground black pepper
    - 1 tablespoon coconut oil

- **Instructions**:

1. Combine turmeric and water in a small saucepan.

2. Cook over low heat, stirring constantly, until a thick paste forms.

3. Stir in black pepper and coconut oil.

4. Allow the paste to cool and store in an airtight container in the refrigerator for up to 2 weeks.

- **Usage**: Use turmeric paste in smoothies, teas, or as a base for curries and sauces.

4. Ginger: Digestive Aid and Immune Booster

Ginger Tea:

- **Ingredients**:
    - 1-2 inches fresh ginger root, peeled and sliced
    - 2 cups water
    - Honey or lemon to taste (optional)

- **Instructions**:

1. Boil ginger slices in water for about 10 minutes.

2. Strain the ginger slices out.

3. Add honey or lemon if desired.

- **Usage**: Drink ginger tea to aid digestion, reduce nausea, or boost the immune system.

Ginger Honey Syrup:

- **Ingredients**:
  - 1 cup honey
  - 1/4 cup fresh ginger, peeled and sliced

- **Instructions**:

1. Combine honey and ginger in a small saucepan.

2. Heat over low heat for 10-15 minutes, allowing the flavors to meld.

3. Strain out the ginger slices.

4. Store the syrup in an airtight container at room temperature.

- **Usage**: Use ginger honey syrup in tea, as a sweetener for recipes, or as a soothing remedy for sore throats.

5. Honey: Healing Wounds and Soothing Sore Throats

Honey Lemon Cough Syrup:

- **Ingredients**:
  - 1/2 cup honey
  - Juice of 1 lemon
  - 1/4 cup warm water

- **Instructions**:

1. Mix honey, lemon juice, and warm water in a bowl until well combined.

2. Store in a clean jar.

- **Usage**: Take 1-2 teaspoons of the syrup as needed for cough relief.

Honey and Cinnamon Paste:

- **Ingredients**:

- o   2 tablespoons honey

- o   1 teaspoon ground cinnamon

- **Instructions**:

1. Mix honey and cinnamon until well combined.

2. Store in an airtight container.

- **Usage**: Apply a thin layer to the skin for a soothing treatment or take 1 teaspoon daily for its health benefits.

6. Apple Cider Vinegar: Detoxification and Weight Management

Apple Cider Vinegar Tonic:

- **Ingredients**:

  - o   1-2 tablespoons apple cider vinegar

  - o   1 cup water

  - o   1 tablespoon honey (optional)

- **Instructions**:

1. Combine apple cider vinegar and water in a glass.

2. Stir in honey if desired.

- **Usage**: Drink this tonic before meals to support digestion and weight management.

ACV Salad Dressing:

- **Ingredients**:

  - o   1/4 cup apple cider vinegar

  - o   1/4 cup olive oil

  - o   1 teaspoon Dijon mustard

  - o   1 clove garlic, minced

  - o   Salt and pepper to taste

- **Instructions**:

1. Whisk together all ingredients in a bowl until well combined.

2. Store in a jar in the refrigerator for up to 1 week.

- **Usage**: Use as a dressing for salads or as a marinade for vegetables.

7. Lemon: Vitamin C Source and Alkalizing Agent

Lemon Water:

- **Ingredients**:
    - Juice of 1 lemon
    - 1 glass of water
- **Instructions**:

1. Squeeze lemon juice into a glass of water.
2. Stir well and drink immediately.

- **Usage**: Start your day with lemon water to support hydration and detoxification.

Lemon and Ginger Smoothie:

- **Ingredients**:
    - Juice of 1 lemon
    - 1-inch piece of fresh ginger, peeled
    - 1 banana
    - 1 cup spinach
    - 1 cup water or coconut water
- **Instructions**:

1. Blend all ingredients until smooth.
2. Pour into a glass and enjoy.

- **Usage**: Enjoy this smoothie as a refreshing and health-boosting drink.

Incorporating these ingredients into your daily routine can offer a range of health benefits, from boosting immune function to supporting digestive health. Each recipe provides a practical way to use these natural remedies in your diet and lifestyle. Experiment with these preparations to find what works best for you and enjoy the enhanced wellness that these powerful ingredients can bring.

Home Remedies for Common Health Issues

Cold and Flu: Natural Remedies for Quick Relief

Cold and flu symptoms can be uncomfortable and disruptive, but natural remedies offer effective ways to alleviate symptoms and support recovery. This section explores various natural treatments and approaches to help manage cold and flu symptoms, focusing on ingredients with proven efficacy and practical applications.

1. Ginger and Honey Tea

Ingredients:

- 1-2 inches fresh ginger root, peeled and sliced
- 1 cup hot water
- 1-2 tablespoons honey
- Lemon juice (optional)

Instructions:

1. Boil ginger slices in water for 10-15 minutes.
2. Strain the ginger out and pour the tea into a cup.
3. Stir in honey and a splash of lemon juice if desired.
4. Drink warm, 2-3 times a day.

Benefits:

- **Ginger**: Acts as an anti-inflammatory and can help soothe a sore throat and reduce coughing. It also aids digestion and supports immune function.
- **Honey**: Soothes the throat and has antimicrobial properties that can help fight infections.

2. Garlic Infused Soup

Ingredients:

- 4-5 cloves garlic, minced

- 1 onion, chopped

- 1 carrot, chopped

- 1 celery stalk, chopped

- 4 cups vegetable or chicken broth

- 1 tablespoon olive oil

- Salt and pepper to taste

- Fresh herbs (optional)

Instructions:

1. Heat olive oil in a pot over medium heat.

2. Sauté garlic, onion, carrot, and celery until soft.

3. Add broth and bring to a boil.

4. Reduce heat and simmer for 20-30 minutes.

5. Season with salt, pepper, and fresh herbs if desired.

6. Serve warm.

Benefits:

- **Garlic**: Known for its antiviral and antibacterial properties, garlic helps boost the immune system and may reduce the severity of cold symptoms.

- **Vegetable Broth**: Provides hydration and essential nutrients, while the warm liquid can help ease congestion.

3. Elderberry Syrup

Ingredients:

- 1 cup dried elderberries

- 3 cups water

- 1 cup honey

- 1 tablespoon fresh ginger (optional)

- 1 cinnamon stick (optional)

Instructions:

1. Combine elderberries, water, and optional ingredients in a pot.

2. Bring to a boil, then reduce heat and simmer for 30-45 minutes.

3. Strain the mixture through a fine mesh sieve.

4. Stir in honey while still warm.

5. Store in a clean jar in the refrigerator for up to 6 weeks.

Benefits:

- **Elderberries**: Rich in antioxidants and vitamins, elderberries are believed to reduce the duration and severity of cold and flu symptoms.

- **Honey**: Adds sweetness and additional soothing properties.

4. Steam Inhalation with Eucalyptus

Ingredients:

- 2-3 drops eucalyptus essential oil

- 1 large bowl

- Hot water

Instructions:

1. Fill a bowl with hot water.

2. Add eucalyptus essential oil to the water.

3. Lean over the bowl, covering your head with a towel to trap the steam.

4. Inhale the steam for 5-10 minutes.

Benefits:

- **Eucalyptus Oil**: Acts as a decongestant and can help relieve sinus congestion and cough.

5. Hot Lemon and Ginger Drink

Ingredients:

- Juice of 1 lemon

- 1-inch piece of fresh ginger, peeled and sliced

- 1 cup hot water

- Honey to taste

Instructions:

1. Boil ginger slices in hot water for 5-10 minutes.

2. Strain the ginger out and add lemon juice and honey to the tea.

3. Drink warm.

Benefits:

- **Lemon**: Provides vitamin C and acts as an immune booster.

- **Ginger**: Offers anti-inflammatory benefits and helps soothe a sore throat.

6. Chamomile Tea with Honey

Ingredients:

- 1 chamomile tea bag

- 1 cup hot water

- 1-2 tablespoons honey

Instructions:

1. Steep the chamomile tea bag in hot water for 5 minutes.

2. Remove the tea bag and stir in honey.

3. Drink warm.

Benefits:

- **Chamomile**: Has calming properties that can help with sleep and relaxation, which is beneficial during illness.

- **Honey**: Provides soothing relief for the throat and adds antimicrobial benefits.

7. Turmeric Milk

Ingredients:

- 1 cup milk (dairy or plant-based)

- 1 teaspoon turmeric powder

- 1/2 teaspoon black pepper

- 1 tablespoon honey or maple syrup

Instructions:

1. Heat milk in a saucepan over medium heat.

2. Stir in turmeric, black pepper, and sweetener.

3. Heat until warm, but not boiling.

4. Drink before bed.

Benefits:

- **Turmeric**: Offers anti-inflammatory and antioxidant properties that can help with symptoms of cold and flu.

- **Black Pepper**: Enhances the absorption of turmeric and adds additional health benefits.

8. Spiced Apple Cider

Ingredients:

- 2 cups apple cider

- 1 cinnamon stick

- 2-3 cloves

- 1-2 slices fresh ginger

Instructions:

1. Heat apple cider in a pot with cinnamon, cloves, and ginger.

2. Simmer for 10-15 minutes.

3. Strain and serve warm.

Benefits:

- **Apple Cider**: Provides hydration and warmth, which can help soothe symptoms.

- **Spices**: Cinnamon, cloves, and ginger add soothing and anti-inflammatory properties.

9. Saltwater Gargle

Ingredients:

- 1/2 teaspoon salt

- 1 cup warm water

Instructions:

1. Dissolve salt in warm water.

2. Gargle with the solution for 30 seconds, then spit out.

3. Repeat 2-3 times a day.

Benefits:

- **Salt**: Helps reduce throat inflammation and can provide temporary relief from a sore throat.

10. Peppermint Tea

Ingredients:

- 1 peppermint tea bag or a handful of fresh peppermint leaves

- 1 cup hot water

- Honey or lemon to taste (optional)

Instructions:

1. Steep peppermint tea bag or leaves in hot water for 5-10 minutes.

2. Remove the tea bag or strain out the leaves.

3. Add honey or lemon if desired.

Benefits:

- **Peppermint**: Acts as a natural decongestant and can help soothe a sore throat and alleviate coughing.

Natural remedies can offer significant relief from cold and flu symptoms, helping to ease discomfort and support recovery. From soothing teas and soups to effective steam inhalations and gargles, these remedies leverage the healing properties of common ingredients to combat illness naturally. While these treatments can be effective, it's important to consult with a healthcare provider for severe or persistent symptoms and to ensure that natural remedies complement any conventional treatments you may be using.

Headaches and Migraines: Herbal Solutions for Pain Management

Headaches and migraines can be debilitating, affecting daily life and well-being. Herbal remedies offer natural approaches to managing these conditions, providing relief and supporting overall health. This section explores effective herbal solutions for headaches and migraines, including their benefits, preparation methods, and practical applications.

1. Peppermint for Tension Headaches

Peppermint Tea:

- **Ingredients**:
    - 1-2 teaspoons dried peppermint leaves or 1 peppermint tea bag
    - 1 cup hot water
    - Honey (optional)
- **Instructions**:
1. Steep peppermint leaves or tea bag in hot water for 5-10 minutes.
2. Strain out the leaves or remove the tea bag.
3. Add honey if desired.
- **Usage**: Drink 1-2 cups of peppermint tea daily to help relieve tension headaches.

Peppermint Oil Massage:

- **Ingredients**:
    - 2-3 drops peppermint essential oil
    - 1 tablespoon carrier oil (e.g., coconut or olive oil)
- **Instructions**:
1. Mix peppermint oil with carrier oil.
2. Gently massage the mixture onto the temples and the back of the neck.
- **Usage**: Apply 2-3 times daily or as needed for headache relief.

Benefits:

- **Peppermint**: Contains menthol, which helps relax muscles and ease tension. It also has cooling properties that can reduce headache pain.

2. Lavender for Migraine Relief

Lavender Tea:

- **Ingredients**:
  - 1-2 teaspoons dried lavender flowers
  - 1 cup hot water
  - Honey (optional)
- **Instructions**:
1. Steep lavender flowers in hot water for 5-10 minutes.
2. Strain out the flowers and add honey if desired.
- **Usage**: Drink 1 cup of lavender tea, especially before bed, to promote relaxation and reduce migraine symptoms.

Lavender Essential Oil Inhalation:

- **Ingredients**:
  - 2-3 drops lavender essential oil
  - 1 bowl of hot water
- **Instructions**:
1. Add lavender oil to a bowl of hot water.
2. Lean over the bowl and cover your head with a towel to inhale the steam for 5-10 minutes.
- **Usage**: Use 1-2 times daily or as needed for migraine relief.

Benefits:

- **Lavender**: Known for its calming and relaxing properties, lavender helps alleviate stress and anxiety, which can be triggers for migraines.

3. Feverfew for Migraine Prevention

Feverfew Tea:

- **Ingredients**:

- 1-2 teaspoons dried feverfew leaves
- 1 cup hot water
- Honey (optional)

- **Instructions**:

1. Steep feverfew leaves in hot water for 5-10 minutes.

2. Strain out the leaves and add honey if desired.

- **Usage**: Drink 1 cup of feverfew tea daily to help prevent migraines.

Feverfew Capsules:

- **Ingredients**:

  - Feverfew capsules (available at health food stores)

- **Instructions**:

1. Follow the dosage instructions on the supplement label.

- **Usage**: Take as directed to help reduce the frequency and severity of migraines.

Benefits:

- **Feverfew**: Contains compounds that inhibit migraine-triggering substances in the body. Regular use may help reduce the frequency and severity of migraines.

4. Ginger for Nausea Associated with Migraines

Ginger Tea:

- **Ingredients**:

  - 1-2 inches fresh ginger root, peeled and sliced
  - 1 cup hot water
  - Honey or lemon (optional)

- **Instructions**:

1. Boil ginger slices in water for 10 minutes.

2. Strain the ginger out and add honey or lemon if desired.

- **Usage**: Drink 1-2 cups of ginger tea to alleviate nausea associated with migraines.

Ginger Powder:

- **Ingredients**:
    - 1/2 teaspoon ginger powder
    - 1 cup warm water
- **Instructions**:

1. Mix ginger powder into warm water.

2. Stir well and drink immediately.

- **Usage**: Take 1-2 times daily to help manage migraine-related nausea.

Benefits:

- **Ginger**: Known for its anti-nausea and anti-inflammatory properties, ginger can help reduce nausea and provide relief during migraine episodes.

5. Willow Bark for Pain Relief

Willow Bark Tea:

- **Ingredients**:
    - 1-2 teaspoons dried willow bark
    - 1 cup hot water
    - Honey (optional)
- **Instructions**:

1. Steep willow bark in hot water for 10-15 minutes.

2. Strain out the bark and add honey if desired.

- **Usage**: Drink 1 cup of willow bark tea 2-3 times a day for pain relief.

Benefits:

- **Willow Bark**: Contains salicin, a compound similar to aspirin, which helps reduce pain and inflammation.

6. Rosemary for Headache Relief

Rosemary Tea:

- **Ingredients**:
    - 1-2 teaspoons dried rosemary leaves

- o 1 cup hot water

- o Honey (optional)

- **Instructions**:

1. Steep rosemary leaves in hot water for 5-10 minutes.

2. Strain out the leaves and add honey if desired.

- **Usage**: Drink 1 cup of rosemary tea to help relieve headaches.

Rosemary Essential Oil:

- **Ingredients**:

  - o 2-3 drops rosemary essential oil

  - o 1 tablespoon carrier oil (e.g., coconut or olive oil)

- **Instructions**:

1. Mix rosemary oil with carrier oil.

2. Massage the mixture onto the temples and the base of the skull.

- **Usage**: Apply 2-3 times daily or as needed for headache relief.

Benefits:

- **Rosemary**: Contains anti-inflammatory and analgesic properties that can help alleviate headache pain and improve circulation.

7. Practical Tips for Using Herbal Remedies

- **Consistency**: For best results, use herbal remedies consistently. Many herbs require regular use to achieve and maintain their benefits.

- **Dosage**: Follow recommended dosages for teas, capsules, and essential oils to avoid potential side effects.

- **Consultation**: If headaches or migraines are severe or persistent, consult with a healthcare provider to rule out underlying conditions and discuss the use of herbal remedies in conjunction with other treatments.

Herbal remedies offer a natural approach to managing headaches and migraines, providing relief and supporting overall well-being. By incorporating herbs such as peppermint, lavender, feverfew, ginger, willow bark, and rosemary into your routine, you can address both the symptoms and potential triggers of headaches and migraines. Experiment with these remedies to find what works best for you and consult with a healthcare provider for personalized advice and treatment options.

Digestive Disorders: Soothing Remedies for Indigestion, Constipation, and Diarrhea

Digestive disorders such as indigestion, constipation, and diarrhea can significantly impact quality of life. Natural remedies offer effective ways to soothe and support the digestive system, addressing symptoms and promoting overall digestive health. This section provides herbal solutions and practical tips for managing these common digestive issues.

1. Indigestion: Remedies to Alleviate Discomfort

Peppermint Tea:

- **Ingredients**:
  - 1-2 teaspoons dried peppermint leaves or 1 peppermint tea bag
  - 1 cup hot water
  - Honey (optional)

- **Instructions**:

1. Steep peppermint leaves or tea bag in hot water for 5-10 minutes.
2. Strain out the leaves or remove the tea bag.
3. Add honey if desired.

- **Usage**: Drink 1-2 cups of peppermint tea after meals to help ease indigestion.

Ginger Tea:

- **Ingredients**:
  - 1-2 inches fresh ginger root, peeled and sliced
  - 1 cup hot water
  - Honey or lemon (optional)

- **Instructions**:

1. Boil ginger slices in hot water for 10 minutes.
2. Strain out the ginger and add honey or lemon if desired.

- **Usage**: Drink 1 cup of ginger tea 2-3 times a day to relieve indigestion.

Chamomile Tea:

- **Ingredients**:
    - 1 chamomile tea bag or 1-2 teaspoons dried chamomile flowers
    - 1 cup hot water
    - Honey (optional)

- **Instructions**:

1. Steep chamomile tea bag or flowers in hot water for 5 minutes.
2. Remove the tea bag or strain out the flowers.
3. Add honey if desired.

- **Usage**: Drink 1 cup of chamomile tea to soothe the digestive tract and reduce inflammation.

Benefits:

- **Peppermint**: Helps relax the muscles of the digestive tract and reduce bloating and gas.
- **Ginger**: Aids digestion and alleviates nausea and discomfort.
- **Chamomile**: Soothes the digestive lining and reduces inflammation.

2. Constipation: Natural Remedies to Promote Regularity

Flaxseed:

- **Ingredients**:
    - 1-2 tablespoons ground flaxseed
    - Water or juice

- **Instructions**:

1. Mix ground flaxseed with water or juice.
2. Drink immediately.

- **Usage**: Consume 1-2 times daily to promote regular bowel movements.

Psyllium Husk:

- **Ingredients**:
    - 1 tablespoon psyllium husk
    - 1 cup water
- **Instructions**:

1. Mix psyllium husk with water and stir well.
2. Drink immediately.

- **Usage**: Take 1-2 times daily to help relieve constipation.

Aloe Vera Juice:

- **Ingredients**:
    - 1/4 cup aloe vera juice
- **Instructions**:

1. Drink aloe vera juice on an empty stomach in the morning.

- **Usage**: Consume 1/4 cup daily to support bowel regularity.

Warm Lemon Water:

- **Ingredients**:
    - Juice of 1 lemon
    - 1 cup warm water
- **Instructions**:

1. Mix lemon juice with warm water.
2. Drink first thing in the morning.

- **Usage**: Drink daily to stimulate digestion and promote regular bowel movements.

Benefits:

- **Flaxseed and Psyllium Husk**: High in fiber, these supplements help add bulk to the stool and promote regularity.
- **Aloe Vera**: Contains natural laxative properties that help alleviate constipation.
- **Lemon**: Stimulates bile production, which aids in digestion and bowel movements.

3. Diarrhea: Remedies to Manage and Rehydrate

Chamomile Tea:

- **Ingredients**:
    - 1 chamomile tea bag or 1-2 teaspoons dried chamomile flowers
    - 1 cup hot water
- **Instructions**:

1. Steep chamomile tea bag or flowers in hot water for 5 minutes.
2. Remove the tea bag or strain out the flowers.

- **Usage**: Drink 1-2 cups of chamomile tea daily to soothe the digestive tract and reduce diarrhea.

Rice Water:

- **Ingredients**:
    - 1/2 cup rice
    - 2 cups water
- **Instructions**:

1. Boil rice in water for 10 minutes.
2. Strain the rice and drink the remaining water.

- **Usage**: Drink 1 cup of rice water 2-3 times a day to help manage diarrhea and rehydrate.

Probiotic-Rich Foods:

- **Ingredients**:
    - Yogurt or kefir with live cultures
- **Instructions**:

1. Consume yogurt or kefir daily.

- **Usage**: Eat 1-2 servings of probiotic-rich foods daily to support gut health and restore balance.

Bananas:

- **Ingredients**:
    - Ripe bananas

- **Instructions**:

1.   Eat 1-2 ripe bananas daily.

- **Usage**: Consume as part of your diet to help firm up stool and provide essential nutrients.

Benefits:

- **Chamomile**: Reduces inflammation and soothes the digestive tract.

- **Rice Water**: Helps rehydrate and provides essential nutrients lost during diarrhea.

- **Probiotics**: Restore beneficial gut bacteria and support digestive health.

- **Bananas**: Provide pectin, which helps absorb excess fluid and firm up stool.

4. Practical Tips for Digestive Health

- **Hydration**: Drink plenty of water throughout the day to support digestion and overall health.

- **Diet**: Incorporate fiber-rich foods, such as fruits, vegetables, and whole grains, into your diet to support regular bowel movements.

- **Avoid Triggers**: Identify and avoid foods or beverages that may trigger digestive issues, such as caffeine, alcohol, or high-fat foods.

- **Consultation**: If digestive symptoms persist or worsen, consult with a healthcare provider to address potential underlying conditions and receive appropriate treatment.

Natural remedies offer effective ways to manage and alleviate digestive disorders such as indigestion, constipation, and diarrhea. By incorporating herbs like peppermint, ginger, chamomile, and probiotics into your routine, you can support digestive health and address common symptoms. Experiment with these remedies to find what works best for you and consult with a healthcare provider for personalized advice and treatment options.

Stress and Anxiety: Calming Herbs for Mental Wellness

Stress and anxiety are prevalent issues that can impact both mental and physical health. Herbal remedies offer natural ways to alleviate stress and anxiety, promoting mental wellness and relaxation. This section explores various herbs known for their calming effects, providing practical applications and preparation methods for effective stress and anxiety relief.

1. Chamomile for Relaxation

Chamomile Tea:

- **Ingredients**:
    - 1 chamomile tea bag or 1-2 teaspoons dried chamomile flowers
    - 1 cup hot water
    - Honey (optional)
- **Instructions**:

1. Steep chamomile tea bag or flowers in hot water for 5 minutes.
2. Remove the tea bag or strain out the flowers.
3. Add honey if desired.

- **Usage**: Drink 1-2 cups of chamomile tea daily, especially before bed, to promote relaxation and reduce anxiety.

Chamomile Extract:

- **Ingredients**:
    - Chamomile tincture (available at health food stores)
- **Instructions**:

1. Follow the dosage instructions on the tincture label.

- **Usage**: Take as directed to help manage stress and anxiety.

Benefits:

- **Chamomile**: Contains calming compounds such as apigenin that help relax the nervous system and promote restful sleep.

2. Lavender for Stress Relief

Lavender Tea:

- **Ingredients**:
    - 1-2 teaspoons dried lavender flowers
    - 1 cup hot water
    - Honey (optional)

- **Instructions**:

1. Steep lavender flowers in hot water for 5 minutes.

2. Strain out the flowers and add honey if desired.

- **Usage**: Drink 1 cup of lavender tea to help alleviate stress and anxiety.

Lavender Essential Oil:

- **Ingredients**:
  - 2-3 drops lavender essential oil
  - 1 tablespoon carrier oil (e.g., coconut or olive oil)

- **Instructions**:

1. Mix lavender oil with carrier oil.

2. Apply to pulse points or diffuse in a room.

- **Usage**: Use as needed for relaxation and to reduce stress levels.

Benefits:

- **Lavender**: Known for its relaxing and mood-enhancing properties, lavender helps reduce anxiety and improve sleep quality.

3. Valerian Root for Anxiety and Sleep

Valerian Root Tea:

- **Ingredients**:
  - 1-2 teaspoons dried valerian root
  - 1 cup hot water

- **Instructions**:

1. Steep valerian root in hot water for 10-15 minutes.

2. Strain out the root.

- **Usage**: Drink 1 cup of valerian root tea before bedtime to promote relaxation and improve sleep quality.

Valerian Root Capsules:

- **Ingredients**:

       o   Valerian root capsules (available at health food stores)

- **Instructions**:

1. Follow the dosage instructions on the supplement label.

- **Usage**: Take as directed, typically in the evening, to support stress relief and improve sleep.

Benefits:

- **Valerian Root**: Contains compounds that act as mild sedatives, helping to reduce anxiety and improve sleep quality.

4. Passionflower for Anxiety Relief

Passionflower Tea:

- **Ingredients**:
  - 1-2 teaspoons dried passionflower
  - 1 cup hot water
  - Honey (optional)

- **Instructions**:

1. Steep passionflower in hot water for 5-10 minutes.

2. Strain out the flowers and add honey if desired.

- **Usage**: Drink 1-2 cups of passionflower tea daily to help alleviate anxiety and promote relaxation.

Passionflower Extract:

- **Ingredients**:
  - Passionflower tincture (available at health food stores)

- **Instructions**:

1. Follow the dosage instructions on the tincture label.

- **Usage**: Take as directed to help manage anxiety.

Benefits:

- **Passionflower**: Known for its calming effects, passionflower helps reduce anxiety and promotes a sense of well-being.

5. Lemon Balm for Stress Reduction

Lemon Balm Tea:

- **Ingredients**:
  - 1-2 teaspoons dried lemon balm leaves
  - 1 cup hot water
  - Honey (optional)
- **Instructions**:
1. Steep lemon balm leaves in hot water for 5-10 minutes.
2. Strain out the leaves and add honey if desired.
- **Usage**: Drink 1-2 cups of lemon balm tea to help reduce stress and anxiety.

Lemon Balm Extract:

- **Ingredients**:
  - Lemon balm tincture (available at health food stores)
- **Instructions**:
1. Follow the dosage instructions on the tincture label.
- **Usage**: Take as directed to support relaxation and stress relief.

Benefits:

- **Lemon Balm**: Contains compounds that have calming effects and can help reduce anxiety and promote mental clarity.

6. Ashwagandha for Stress Adaptation

Ashwagandha Capsules:

- **Ingredients**:
  - Ashwagandha capsules (available at health food stores)
- **Instructions**:
1. Follow the dosage instructions on the supplement label.
- **Usage**: Take as directed to help manage stress and support overall well-being.

Ashwagandha Powder:

- **Ingredients**:
  - 1 teaspoon ashwagandha powder
  - Smoothie or warm milk
- **Instructions**:
1. Mix ashwagandha powder into a smoothie or warm milk.
- **Usage**: Consume daily to support stress reduction and improve resilience.

Benefits:

- **Ashwagandha**: An adaptogen that helps the body adapt to stress and supports overall mental health.

7. Practical Tips for Managing Stress and Anxiety

- **Consistency**: For best results, use herbal remedies regularly and incorporate them into your daily routine.
- **Lifestyle**: Combine herbal remedies with stress-reducing practices such as exercise, meditation, and adequate sleep.
- **Dosage**: Follow recommended dosages for teas, capsules, and extracts to avoid potential side effects.
- **Consultation**: If stress or anxiety are severe or persistent, consult with a healthcare provider for personalized advice and treatment options.

Herbal remedies offer a natural approach to managing stress and anxiety, supporting mental wellness and relaxation. By incorporating herbs such as chamomile, lavender, valerian root, passionflower, lemon balm, and ashwagandha into your routine, you can alleviate stress and anxiety and improve overall well-being. Experiment with these remedies to find what works best for you and consult with a healthcare provider for personalized advice and treatment options.

Sleep Disorders: Natural Ways to Improve Sleep Quality

Sleep disorders can significantly impact daily life, affecting energy levels, mood, and overall health. Natural remedies offer effective ways to improve sleep quality and support restful sleep. This section explores various herbs and practices known for their sleep-enhancing properties, providing practical applications and preparation methods for better sleep.

1. Valerian Root for Better Sleep

Valerian Root Tea:

- **Ingredients**:
    - 1-2 teaspoons dried valerian root
    - 1 cup hot water
- **Instructions**:
1. Steep valerian root in hot water for 10-15 minutes.
2. Strain out the root.
    - **Usage**: Drink 1 cup of valerian root tea 30 minutes to an hour before bedtime.

Valerian Root Capsules:

- **Ingredients**:
    - Valerian root capsules (available at health food stores)
- **Instructions**:
1. Follow the dosage instructions on the supplement label.
    - **Usage**: Take as directed, typically in the evening, to support sleep.

Benefits:

- **Valerian Root**: Contains compounds that act as mild sedatives, helping to relax the nervous system and improve sleep quality.

2. Chamomile for Relaxation

Chamomile Tea:

- **Ingredients**:
    - 1 chamomile tea bag or 1-2 teaspoons dried chamomile flowers
    - 1 cup hot water
    - Honey (optional)
- **Instructions**:
1. Steep chamomile tea bag or flowers in hot water for 5 minutes.
2. Remove the tea bag or strain out the flowers.

3.   Add honey if desired.

- **Usage**: Drink 1-2 cups of chamomile tea in the evening, especially before bed.

Chamomile Extract:

- **Ingredients**:

  - Chamomile tincture (available at health food stores)

- **Instructions**:

1.   Follow the dosage instructions on the tincture label.

- **Usage**: Take as directed to support relaxation and improve sleep.

Benefits:

- **Chamomile**: Contains calming compounds such as apigenin that help relax the mind and body, promoting restful sleep.

3. Lavender for Sleep Enhancement

Lavender Tea:

- **Ingredients**:

  - 1-2 teaspoons dried lavender flowers

  - 1 cup hot water

  - Honey (optional)

- **Instructions**:

1.   Steep lavender flowers in hot water for 5 minutes.

2.   Strain out the flowers and add honey if desired.

- **Usage**: Drink 1 cup of lavender tea before bedtime to promote relaxation and improve sleep quality.

Lavender Essential Oil:

- **Ingredients**:

  - 2-3 drops lavender essential oil

  - 1 tablespoon carrier oil (e.g., coconut or olive oil)

- **Instructions**:

1. Mix lavender oil with carrier oil.

2. Apply to pulse points or diffuse in the bedroom.

- **Usage**: Use as needed to help relax before bed and improve sleep quality.

Benefits:

- **Lavender**: Known for its calming and soothing effects, lavender helps reduce anxiety and promotes a peaceful sleep environment.

4. Passionflower for Sleep Support

Passionflower Tea:

- **Ingredients**:
    o   1-2 teaspoons dried passionflower
    o   1 cup hot water
    o   Honey (optional)

- **Instructions**:

1. Steep passionflower in hot water for 5-10 minutes.

2. Strain out the flowers and add honey if desired.

- **Usage**: Drink 1 cup of passionflower tea before bedtime to help relax and support sleep.

Passionflower Extract:

- **Ingredients**:
    o   Passionflower tincture (available at health food stores)

- **Instructions**:

1. Follow the dosage instructions on the tincture label.

- **Usage**: Take as directed to promote relaxation and improve sleep quality.

Benefits:

- **Passionflower**: Contains compounds that have calming effects, reducing anxiety and promoting restful sleep.

5. Melatonin for Sleep Regulation

Melatonin Supplements:

- **Ingredients**:
  - Melatonin tablets or capsules (available at health food stores)
- **Instructions**:

1. Follow the dosage instructions on the supplement label.

- **Usage**: Take 30 minutes before bedtime to support the body's natural sleep-wake cycle.

Benefits:

- **Melatonin**: A hormone that helps regulate the sleep-wake cycle, melatonin supplements can aid in falling asleep and improving sleep quality.

6. Magnesium for Relaxation

Magnesium Supplements:

- **Ingredients**:
  - Magnesium tablets or capsules (available at health food stores)
- **Instructions**:

1. Follow the dosage instructions on the supplement label.

- **Usage**: Take in the evening to support relaxation and improve sleep quality.

Magnesium-Rich Foods:

- **Ingredients**:
  - Foods such as almonds, spinach, and bananas
- **Instructions**:

1. Incorporate magnesium-rich foods into your diet.

- **Usage**: Eat regularly to support overall relaxation and sleep quality.

Benefits:

- **Magnesium**: Helps relax muscles and nerves, and can aid in falling asleep and improving sleep quality.

7. Practical Tips for Better Sleep

- **Consistency**: Maintain a regular sleep schedule by going to bed and waking up at the same time every day.

- **Sleep Environment**: Create a restful sleep environment by keeping your bedroom dark, cool, and quiet.

- **Relaxation Techniques**: Incorporate relaxation techniques such as deep breathing, meditation, or progressive muscle relaxation before bed.

- **Avoid Stimulants**: Limit caffeine, nicotine, and heavy meals close to bedtime.

- **Screen Time**: Reduce exposure to screens (phones, tablets, computers) at least an hour before bed to promote natural melatonin production.

Natural remedies offer effective ways to improve sleep quality and support restful sleep. By incorporating herbs such as valerian root, chamomile, lavender, passionflower, and melatonin into your routine, along with magnesium and practical sleep-enhancing practices, you can address common sleep issues and promote overall well-being. Experiment with these remedies to find what works best for you and consult with a healthcare provider for personalized advice and treatment options.

Skin Conditions: Topical Treatments for Acne, Eczema, and Rashes

Skin conditions such as acne, eczema, and rashes can cause significant discomfort and impact self-esteem. Natural, topical treatments can help alleviate symptoms and promote healthier skin. This section provides detailed information on effective herbal remedies and treatments for these common skin issues.

1. Acne: Herbal Solutions for Clearer Skin

Tea Tree Oil:

- **Ingredients**:
    - 1-2 drops tea tree oil
    - 1 teaspoon carrier oil (e.g., coconut oil, jojoba oil)

- **Instructions**:

1. Mix tea tree oil with carrier oil.

2. Apply the mixture directly to acne spots using a cotton swab.

- **Usage**: Apply 1-2 times daily to affected areas.

Aloe Vera Gel:

- **Ingredients**:
  - Fresh aloe vera gel (from the plant) or store-bought aloe vera gel
- **Instructions**:
1. Apply a thin layer of aloe vera gel directly to the acne-affected areas.
2. Leave it on for 15-20 minutes, then rinse off with lukewarm water.
- **Usage**: Use 1-2 times daily for best results.

Green Tea Extract:

- **Ingredients**:
  - Green tea extract (available in liquid or cream form)
- **Instructions**:
1. Apply green tea extract to affected areas.
- **Usage**: Apply 1-2 times daily.

Benefits:

- **Tea Tree Oil**: Contains antimicrobial properties that help reduce acne-causing bacteria and inflammation.
- **Aloe Vera**: Soothes the skin, reduces inflammation, and helps in healing acne lesions.
- **Green Tea Extract**: Rich in antioxidants and anti-inflammatory properties that help reduce acne and improve skin health.

2. Eczema: Soothing Remedies for Dry, Itchy Skin

Oatmeal Bath:

- **Ingredients**:
  - 1 cup finely ground oatmeal
  - Warm bath water
- **Instructions**:
1. Add finely ground oatmeal to a warm bath.
2. Soak in the oatmeal bath for 15-20 minutes.
- **Usage**: Use 2-3 times a week to soothe eczema symptoms.

Coconut Oil:

- **Ingredients:**
    - Virgin coconut oil

- **Instructions:**

1. Apply a thin layer of coconut oil directly to eczema patches.

- **Usage:** Apply 2-3 times daily to moisturize and soothe affected areas.

Calendula Cream:

- **Ingredients:**
    - Calendula cream (available at health food stores)

- **Instructions:**

1. Apply calendula cream to eczema patches.

- **Usage:** Use 2-3 times daily to reduce inflammation and itching.

Benefits:

- **Oatmeal:** Contains anti-inflammatory properties and helps soothe dry, itchy skin.
- **Coconut Oil:** Provides deep hydration and reduces inflammation and itching.
- **Calendula:** Known for its soothing and healing properties, helps reduce inflammation and promote skin repair.

3. Rashes: Natural Treatments for Relief

Chamomile Compress:

- **Ingredients:**
    - 1-2 chamomile tea bags
    - 1 cup hot water

- **Instructions:**

1. Steep chamomile tea bags in hot water for 5 minutes.
2. Let the tea cool slightly, then soak a clean cloth in the tea.
3. Apply the cloth as a compress to the rash for 15 minutes.

- **Usage:** Use 1-2 times daily to soothe rashes.

Witch Hazel:

- **Ingredients**:
    - Witch hazel extract (available in liquid form)
- **Instructions**:
1. Apply witch hazel directly to the rash using a cotton ball.
- **Usage**: Apply 2-3 times daily to reduce itching and inflammation.

Aloe Vera and Tea Tree Oil Blend:

- **Ingredients**:
    - 1 tablespoon aloe vera gel
    - 1-2 drops tea tree oil
- **Instructions**:
1. Mix aloe vera gel with tea tree oil.
2. Apply the mixture to the rash.
- **Usage**: Apply 1-2 times daily.

Benefits:

- **Chamomile**: Contains anti-inflammatory and soothing properties that help reduce irritation and redness.
- **Witch Hazel**: Acts as astringent and anti-inflammatory, helping to reduce swelling and itching.
- **Aloe Vera and Tea Tree Oil**: Aloe vera soothes the skin, while tea tree oil provides antimicrobial and anti-inflammatory effects.

4. Practical Tips for Skin Health

- **Patch Test**: Before using any new herbal treatment, perform a patch test on a small area of skin to check for any allergic reactions.
- **Consistency**: For best results, use herbal treatments consistently and as directed.
- **Hydration**: Drink plenty of water to keep the skin hydrated and support overall skin health.
- **Avoid Irritants**: Identify and avoid skincare products or substances that may trigger or worsen skin conditions.

Natural, topical treatments offer effective ways to manage and alleviate symptoms of acne, eczema, and rashes. By incorporating herbs and remedies such as tea tree oil, aloe vera, oatmeal, coconut oil, chamomile, witch hazel, and calendula into your skincare routine, you can address common skin issues and promote healthier, more comfortable skin. Experiment with these remedies to find what works best for you and consult with a healthcare provider for personalized advice and treatment options.

Joint and Muscle Pain: Anti-Inflammatory Remedies for Pain Relief

Joint and muscle pain can be debilitating, affecting mobility and quality of life. Natural remedies offer effective ways to manage pain and inflammation, supporting overall joint and muscle health. This section explores various herbal and natural treatments known for their anti-inflammatory properties, providing practical applications and preparation methods for pain relief.

1. Turmeric for Pain and Inflammation

Turmeric Tea:

- **Ingredients**:
    - 1 teaspoon ground turmeric
    - 1 cup hot water
    - Honey and lemon (optional)

- **Instructions**:

1. Stir ground turmeric into hot water.

2. Let it steep for 5-10 minutes, then strain if needed.

3. Add honey and lemon for flavor if desired.

- **Usage**: Drink 1-2 cups daily to help reduce inflammation and pain.

Turmeric Paste:

- **Ingredients**:
    - 1 tablespoon ground turmeric
    - 1 tablespoon coconut oil

        ◦   A pinch of black pepper

- **Instructions**:

1.   Mix turmeric, coconut oil, and black pepper to form a paste.

2.   Apply the paste directly to the affected joint or muscle.

- **Usage**: Apply 1-2 times daily, leaving it on for 20-30 minutes before rinsing off.

Benefits:

- **Turmeric**: Contains curcumin, a powerful anti-inflammatory compound that helps reduce pain and inflammation.

2. Ginger for Joint and Muscle Pain

Ginger Tea:

- **Ingredients**:

    ◦   1-2 inches fresh ginger root, sliced

    ◦   1 cup hot water

    ◦   Honey (optional)

- **Instructions**:

1.   Steep ginger slices in hot water for 10 minutes.

2.   Strain the ginger and add honey if desired.

- **Usage**: Drink 1-2 cups daily to help manage pain and inflammation.

Ginger Compress:

- **Ingredients**:

    ◦   2 tablespoons ground ginger

    ◦   1/2 cup warm water

- **Instructions**:

1.   Mix ground ginger with warm water to form a paste.

2.   Apply the paste to the affected area using a cloth or gauze.

- **Usage**: Apply the ginger compress 1-2 times daily for 15-20 minutes.

Benefits:

- **Ginger**: Contains gingerol, an anti-inflammatory compound that helps reduce pain and inflammation.

3. Arnica for Bruising and Pain Relief

Arnica Cream:

- **Ingredients**:
    - Arnica cream (available at health food stores)
- **Instructions**:
1. Apply a thin layer of arnica cream to the affected area.
- **Usage**: Apply 2-3 times daily to help reduce pain, bruising, and inflammation.

Arnica Oil:

- **Ingredients**:
    - Arnica-infused oil (available at health food stores)
- **Instructions**:
1. Gently massage arnica oil into the affected area.
- **Usage**: Use 2-3 times daily for relief from muscle pain and bruising.

Benefits:

- **Arnica**: Known for its anti-inflammatory and pain-relieving properties, arnica helps reduce bruising and sore muscles.

4. Epsom Salt for Muscle Relaxation

Epsom Salt Bath:

- **Ingredients**:
    - 2 cups Epsom salt
    - Warm bath water
- **Instructions**:
1. Dissolve Epsom salt in warm bath water.
2. Soak in the bath for 15-20 minutes.
- **Usage**: Use 2-3 times a week to help relax muscles and alleviate pain.

Benefits:

- **Epsom Salt**: Contains magnesium, which helps relax muscles and reduce inflammation.

5. Willow Bark for Pain Relief

Willow Bark Tea:

- **Ingredients**:

  - 1-2 teaspoons dried willow bark

  - 1 cup hot water

- **Instructions**:

1. Steep willow bark in hot water for 10-15 minutes.

2. Strain out the bark.

- **Usage**: Drink 1-2 cups daily to help manage joint and muscle pain.

Benefits:

- **Willow Bark**: Contains salicin, a compound similar to aspirin, which helps reduce pain and inflammation.

6. Peppermint Oil for Pain Relief

Peppermint Oil Massage:

- **Ingredients**:

  - 2-3 drops peppermint essential oil

  - 1 tablespoon carrier oil (e.g., coconut oil)

- **Instructions**:

1. Mix peppermint oil with carrier oil.

2. Gently massage the mixture into the affected area.

- **Usage**: Apply 2-3 times daily to help alleviate pain and muscle tension.

Benefits:

- **Peppermint Oil**: Contains menthol, which has cooling and analgesic effects that help relieve muscle pain and tension.

7. Practical Tips for Managing Joint and Muscle Pain

- **Consistency**: For best results, use herbal treatments regularly and as directed.

- **Exercise**: Incorporate low-impact exercises, such as swimming or walking, to maintain joint and muscle flexibility.

- **Heat and Cold Therapy**: Alternate between heat and cold packs to reduce inflammation and ease pain.

- **Hydration**: Drink plenty of water to support overall joint health and reduce muscle cramping.

Natural remedies offer effective ways to manage joint and muscle pain, supporting overall health and well-being. By incorporating herbs and treatments such as turmeric, ginger, arnica, Epsom salt, willow bark, and peppermint oil into your routine, you can address pain and inflammation and improve mobility. Experiment with these remedies to find what works best for you and consult with a healthcare provider for personalized advice and treatment options.

Women's Health: Remedies for Menstrual Cramps, Menopause, and Hormonal Balance

Women's health encompasses a range of issues from menstrual cramps to menopause and hormonal imbalances. Natural remedies can provide relief and support for these common concerns. This section explores various herbal and lifestyle treatments to address menstrual cramps, manage menopause symptoms, and maintain hormonal balance.

1. Menstrual Cramps: Easing Pain and Discomfort

Cramp Bark Tea:

- **Ingredients**:
    - 1-2 teaspoons dried cramp bark
    - 1 cup hot water

- **Instructions**:

1. Steep cramp bark in hot water for 10-15 minutes.

2. Strain out the bark.

- **Usage**: Drink 1-2 cups daily during menstruation to help alleviate cramps.

Ginger Tea:

- **Ingredients**:
    - 1-2 inches fresh ginger root, sliced
    - 1 cup hot water
    - Honey (optional)
- **Instructions**:

1. Steep ginger slices in hot water for 10 minutes.

2. Strain the ginger and add honey if desired.

- **Usage**: Drink 1-2 cups daily, especially during menstruation.

Benefits:

- **Cramp Bark**: Contains antispasmodic properties that help reduce uterine contractions and alleviate menstrual cramps.
- **Ginger**: Contains anti-inflammatory compounds that help relieve pain and reduce menstrual discomfort.

Heating Pads:

- **Instructions**:
    1. Apply a heating pad to the lower abdomen for 15-20 minutes.
- **Usage**: Use as needed during menstruation to help relax muscles and ease pain.

Benefits:

- **Heating Pads**: Provide soothing relief by increasing blood flow and relaxing muscle tension.

2. Menopause: Managing Symptoms and Improving Quality of Life

Black Cohosh:

- **Ingredients**:
    - Black cohosh capsules or tincture (available at health food stores)
- **Instructions**:

1. Follow the dosage instructions on the supplement label or tincture.

- **Usage**: Take as directed to help manage menopause symptoms such as hot flashes and mood swings.

Red Clover Tea:

- **Ingredients**:
    - 1-2 teaspoons dried red clover flowers
    - 1 cup hot water
- **Instructions**:
1. Steep red clover flowers in hot water for 10 minutes.
2. Strain out the flowers.
- **Usage**: Drink 1-2 cups daily to support hormonal balance during menopause.

Benefits:

- **Black Cohosh**: Contains phytoestrogens that help alleviate hot flashes, mood swings, and other menopause symptoms.
- **Red Clover**: Contains isoflavones, plant-based compounds that help balance hormones and ease menopause symptoms.

Evening Primrose Oil:

- **Ingredients**:
    - Evening primrose oil capsules (available at health food stores)
- **Instructions**:
1. Follow the dosage instructions on the supplement label.
- **Usage**: Take as directed to support hormonal balance and reduce menopausal symptoms.

Benefits:

- **Evening Primrose Oil**: Contains gamma-linolenic acid (GLA), which helps regulate hormone levels and improve skin health during menopause.

3. Hormonal Balance: Supporting Overall Well-Being

Chaste Tree (Vitex):

- **Ingredients**:
    - Chaste tree capsules or tincture (available at health food stores)
- **Instructions**:

1.   Follow the dosage instructions on the supplement label or tincture.

- **Usage**: Take as directed to support hormonal balance and alleviate symptoms of PMS and irregular cycles.

Ashwagandha:

- **Ingredients**:

  o   Ashwagandha capsules or powder (available at health food stores)

- **Instructions**:

1.   Follow the dosage instructions on the supplement label or mix powder into a smoothie.

- **Usage**: Take as directed to help manage stress and support hormonal balance.

Benefits:

- **Chaste Tree**: Helps regulate menstrual cycles and alleviate symptoms of PMS by balancing hormones.

- **Ashwagandha**: An adaptogen that helps manage stress, which can affect hormonal balance.

Lifestyle Tips for Hormonal Balance:

- **Balanced Diet**: Include a diet rich in fruits, vegetables, whole grains, and lean proteins to support overall health and hormonal balance.

- **Regular Exercise**: Engage in regular physical activity to help regulate hormones and improve mood.

- **Stress Management**: Incorporate stress-reducing practices such as yoga, meditation, or deep breathing exercises into your daily routine.

- **Adequate Sleep**: Ensure 7-9 hours of quality sleep per night to support hormonal health and overall well-being.

Natural remedies offer valuable support for managing menstrual cramps, menopause symptoms, and hormonal balance. By incorporating herbs such as cramp bark, ginger, black cohosh, red clover, evening primrose oil, chaste tree, and ashwagandha into your routine, along with adopting a balanced lifestyle, you can address common women's health issues and enhance overall well-being. Experiment with these remedies to find what works best for you and consult with a healthcare provider for personalized advice and treatment options.

Men's Health: Enhancing Prostate Health and Libido Naturally

Men's health concerns, such as prostate health and libido, can significantly impact quality of life. Natural remedies offer effective ways to support prostate function and enhance sexual vitality. This section explores various herbal and lifestyle treatments that promote prostate health and improve libido naturally.

1. Prostate Health: Supporting Function and Reducing Symptoms

Saw Palmetto:

- **Ingredients**:
    - Saw palmetto capsules or tincture (available at health food stores)
- **Instructions**:
1. Follow the dosage instructions on the supplement label or tincture.
- **Usage**: Take as directed to support prostate health and reduce symptoms of benign prostatic hyperplasia (BPH).

Benefits:

- **Saw Palmetto**: Contains compounds that may help reduce prostate enlargement and improve urinary symptoms associated with BPH.

Pumpkin Seed Oil:

- **Ingredients**:
    - Pumpkin seed oil capsules or liquid form (available at health food stores)
- **Instructions**:
1. Follow the dosage instructions on the supplement label.
- **Usage**: Take as directed to support prostate health and reduce symptoms of BPH.

Benefits:

- **Pumpkin Seed Oil**: Rich in zinc and phytosterols, which may help maintain prostate health and support urinary function.

Pygeum:

- **Ingredients**:

- Pygeum capsules or tincture (available at health food stores)
- **Instructions**:
1. Follow the dosage instructions on the supplement label or tincture.
- **Usage**: Take as directed to help alleviate symptoms of BPH and support overall prostate health.

Benefits:

- **Pygeum**: Derived from the African plum tree, pygeum may help reduce urinary symptoms associated with prostate enlargement and support overall prostate function.

Nettle Root:

- **Ingredients**:
    - Nettle root capsules or tincture (available at health food stores)
- **Instructions**:
1. Follow the dosage instructions on the supplement label or tincture.
- **Usage**: Take as directed to support prostate health and reduce urinary symptoms.

Benefits:

- **Nettle Root**: May help reduce symptoms of BPH and improve urinary flow by supporting prostate function.

2. Libido Enhancement: Boosting Sexual Vitality Naturally

Tribulus Terrestris:

- **Ingredients**:
    - Tribulus terrestris capsules or tincture (available at health food stores)
- **Instructions**:
1. Follow the dosage instructions on the supplement label or tincture.
- **Usage**: Take as directed to support libido and enhance sexual function.

Benefits:

- **Tribulus Terrestris**: Known for its potential to enhance sexual desire and improve overall sexual health by supporting testosterone levels.

Maca Root:

- **Ingredients:**
    - Maca root powder or capsules (available at health food stores)
- **Instructions:**

1. Mix maca root powder into smoothies or take capsules as directed.

- **Usage**: Take as directed to improve libido, stamina, and overall sexual vitality.

Benefits:

- **Maca Root**: Known for its adaptogenic properties that help balance hormones, improve energy levels, and support sexual health.

Ginseng:

- **Ingredients:**
    - Ginseng capsules or tincture (available at health food stores)
- **Instructions:**

1. Follow the dosage instructions on the supplement label or tincture.

- **Usage**: Take as directed to enhance sexual function and overall vitality.

Benefits:

- **Ginseng**: An adaptogen that helps improve energy, reduce stress, and enhance sexual performance.

L-Arginine:

- **Ingredients:**
    - L-arginine capsules or powder (available at health food stores)
- **Instructions:**

1. Follow the dosage instructions on the supplement label or mix powder into smoothies.

- **Usage**: Take as directed to support erectile function and improve sexual health.

Benefits:

- **L-Arginine**: An amino acid that helps increase nitric oxide levels, improving blood flow and supporting erectile function.

3. Lifestyle Tips for Optimal Prostate Health and Libido

- **Balanced Diet**: Include a diet rich in fruits, vegetables, whole grains, and lean proteins to support overall health and hormone balance. Foods rich in antioxidants, such as tomatoes (lycopene), and zinc-rich foods, such as nuts and seeds, support prostate health.

- **Regular Exercise**: Engage in regular physical activity, including cardiovascular and strength training exercises, to maintain overall health and improve libido.

- **Stress Management**: Incorporate stress-reducing practices such as yoga, meditation, or deep breathing exercises to support hormone balance and sexual health.

- **Adequate Sleep**: Ensure 7-9 hours of quality sleep per night to support overall health, hormone production, and sexual vitality.

Natural remedies and lifestyle changes offer valuable support for enhancing prostate health and boosting libido. By incorporating herbs such as saw palmetto, pumpkin seed oil, pygeum, nettle root, tribulus terrestris, maca root, ginseng, and L-arginine into your routine, along with adopting a balanced diet, regular exercise, and stress management practices, you can promote overall well-being and improve sexual health. Experiment with these remedies to find what works best for you and consult with a healthcare provider for personalized advice and treatment options.

Child-Friendly Remedies: Safe and Gentle Solutions for Common Ailments

Children often experience various ailments, from colds and flu to minor injuries and digestive issues. Natural remedies can provide gentle, effective relief while minimizing the use of pharmaceuticals. This section explores safe and child-friendly remedies for common ailments, focusing on natural treatments that are appropriate for young ones.

1. Cold and Flu: Natural Remedies for Quick Relief

Honey Lemon Tea:

- **Ingredients**:
    - 1 teaspoon honey
    - Juice of half a lemon
    - 1 cup warm water

- **Instructions**:
1. Stir honey and lemon juice into warm water until well mixed.
    - **Usage**: Give 1-2 teaspoons of the mixture to children 2 years and older, up to 3 times a day.

Benefits:

- **Honey**: Soothes sore throats and has mild antibacterial properties.
- **Lemon**: Provides vitamin C and helps boost the immune system.

Ginger Tea:

- **Ingredients**:
    - 1 small piece of fresh ginger, sliced
    - 1 cup warm water
    - Honey (optional, for children over 1 year)
- **Instructions**:
1. Steep ginger slices in warm water for 5-10 minutes.
2. Strain and add honey if desired.
    - **Usage**: Give 1-2 teaspoons of the tea to children 2 years and older.

Benefits:

- **Ginger**: Helps with nausea and has anti-inflammatory properties that can soothe sore throats.

Steam Inhalation:

- **Ingredients**:
    - A bowl of hot water
    - A few drops of eucalyptus or lavender essential oil (optional)
- **Instructions**:
1. Place the child in a safe position with a bowl of hot water in front of them.
2. Have them breathe in the steam for 5-10 minutes.
    - **Usage**: Use once or twice a day to help with congestion.

Benefits:

- **Steam**: Helps loosen mucus and ease breathing.

2. Digestive Disorders: Soothing Remedies for Indigestion, Constipation, and Diarrhea

Chamomile Tea:

- **Ingredients:**

    o   1 teaspoon dried chamomile flowers

    o   1 cup hot water

- **Instructions:**

1.   Steep chamomile flowers in hot water for 5-10 minutes.

2.   Strain before serving.

- **Usage**: Give 1-2 teaspoons of the tea to children 2 years and older.

Benefits:

- **Chamomile**: Has calming effects and can help with digestive issues and relaxation.

Prune Juice:

- **Ingredients:**

    o   100% pure prune juice (no added sugars)

- **Instructions:**

1.   Offer 1-2 tablespoons of prune juice to children for constipation relief.

- **Usage**: Use once daily as needed.

Benefits:

- **Prune Juice**: Acts as a natural laxative and helps relieve constipation.

Ginger Ale:

- **Ingredients:**

    o   Flat, caffeine-free ginger ale

- **Instructions:**

1.   Serve a small amount of flat ginger ale to help with nausea.

- **Usage**: Offer 1-2 ounces to children 2 years and older.

Benefits:

- **Ginger Ale**: Ginger helps with nausea and settling the stomach.

3. Skin Conditions: Topical Treatments for Rashes and Minor Cuts

Aloe Vera Gel:

- **Ingredients**:
  - o Fresh aloe vera gel or store-bought pure aloe gel
- **Instructions**:

1. Apply a thin layer of aloe vera gel to the affected area.

- **Usage**: Use as needed for soothing minor rashes and cuts.

Benefits:

- **Aloe Vera**: Provides cooling relief and helps heal minor skin irritations.

Oatmeal Bath:

- **Ingredients**:
  - o 1 cup colloidal oatmeal
- **Instructions**:

1. Add colloidal oatmeal to a warm bath and stir.

- **Usage**: Soak the child in the bath for 10-15 minutes, 1-2 times a day.

Benefits:

- **Oatmeal**: Soothes itchy and irritated skin, especially useful for eczema and rashes.

Calendula Cream:

- **Ingredients**:
  - o Calendula cream or ointment (available at health food stores)
- **Instructions**:

1. Apply a thin layer of calendula cream to the affected area.

- **Usage**: Use 1-2 times daily to help with minor cuts and skin irritations.

Benefits:

- **Calendula**: Known for its anti-inflammatory and healing properties, making it effective for minor skin issues.

4. Earaches: Gentle Remedies for Pain Relief

Warm Compress:

- **Ingredients**:
  - A clean cloth
  - Warm water
- **Instructions**:

1.   Soak the cloth in warm water, wring out excess water, and place it over the affected ear.

- **Usage**: Apply for 10-15 minutes as needed.

Benefits:

- **Warm Compress**: Helps alleviate pain and discomfort by increasing blood flow to the area.

Garlic Oil Drops:

- **Ingredients**:
  - Garlic oil (available at health food stores)
- **Instructions**:

1.   Warm the garlic oil slightly (ensure it is not hot).

2.   Place 1-2 drops in the affected ear.

- **Usage**: Use once or twice daily as needed for earache relief.

Benefits:

- **Garlic Oil**: Known for its antibacterial properties and can help soothe ear discomfort.

5. General Tips for Using Natural Remedies for Children

- **Consult a Pediatrician**: Always check with a healthcare provider before using new remedies, especially for infants and young children.

- **Use Age-Appropriate Dosages**: Adjust dosages according to the child's age and weight.

- **Monitor for Allergic Reactions**: Watch for any adverse reactions or allergies when using new treatments.

- **Maintain Good Hygiene**: Ensure cleanliness when applying topical treatments to prevent infections.

Natural remedies can offer gentle and effective relief for common childhood ailments. By using remedies such as honey lemon tea, chamomile tea, aloe vera gel, and warm compresses, parents can provide soothing care for their children. Always consult with a healthcare provider before starting any new treatment to ensure it is safe and appropriate for your child's specific needs.

Creating Your Herbal Apothecary

Essential Herbs to Keep in Your Home

Having a selection of essential herbs on hand can be incredibly useful for addressing common health issues, enhancing your meals, and supporting overall well-being. Below are some of the most versatile and beneficial herbs to keep in your home, along with their uses and benefits.

1. Peppermint (Mentha × piperita)

Uses:

- **Digestive Aid**: Peppermint tea can soothe indigestion, nausea, and bloating.
- **Headache Relief**: A few drops of peppermint essential oil can be applied to the temples to relieve headaches.
- **Respiratory Health**: Inhalation of peppermint steam can help with congestion and respiratory issues.

Benefits:

- **Menthol**: Provides a cooling sensation and helps relax digestive muscles.
- **Antimicrobial Properties**: Helps fight off pathogens and can soothe sore throats.

2. Chamomile (Matricaria chamomilla)

Uses:

- **Sleep Aid**: Chamomile tea is known for its calming effects and can help improve sleep quality.
- **Digestive Health**: Helps relieve indigestion and bloating.
- **Skin Care**: Chamomile can be used topically to soothe skin irritations and rashes.

Benefits:

- **Apigenin**: An antioxidant that promotes relaxation and can aid in sleep.
- **Anti-inflammatory**: Helps reduce inflammation and soothe the digestive tract.

3. Ginger (Zingiber officinale)

Uses:

- **Nausea Relief**: Ginger tea or ginger ale can help with nausea and motion sickness.
- **Digestive Aid**: Stimulates digestion and can relieve indigestion and bloating.
- **Anti-inflammatory**: Used to reduce inflammation and pain.

Benefits:

- **Gingerol**: A potent compound with anti-inflammatory and antioxidant properties.
- **Digestive Support**: Helps stimulate digestive enzymes and improve overall digestion.

4. Turmeric (Curcuma longa)

Uses:

- **Anti-inflammatory**: Turmeric can be used to reduce inflammation in conditions like arthritis.
- **Digestive Health**: Supports digestion and liver function.
- **Skin Care**: Applied topically, turmeric can help with acne and skin discolorations.

Benefits:

- **Curcumin**: The active ingredient with powerful anti-inflammatory and antioxidant effects.
- **Immune Support**: Helps strengthen the immune system.

5. Lavender (Lavandula angustifolia)

Uses:

- **Stress Relief**: Lavender essential oil can be used in aromatherapy to reduce stress and anxiety.
- **Sleep Aid**: Lavender sachets or essential oil can promote better sleep.
- **Skin Care**: Lavender oil can be applied to minor burns and insect bites for its soothing effects.

Benefits:

- **Linalool**: A compound that has calming and anxiety-reducing effects.
- **Antimicrobial Properties**: Helps prevent infections and can be used to treat minor wounds.

6. Echinacea (Echinacea purpurea)

Uses:

- **Immune Support**: Echinacea is often used to boost the immune system and reduce the duration of colds.
- **Wound Healing**: Applied topically to help heal minor cuts and wounds.

Benefits:

- **Polysaccharides**: Support immune function and help fight infections.
- **Anti-inflammatory**: Helps reduce inflammation and support the healing process.

7. Thyme (Thymus vulgaris)

Uses:

- **Respiratory Health**: Thyme tea or steam can help relieve coughs and bronchitis.
- **Antiseptic**: Thyme can be used as a natural disinfectant for minor cuts and scrapes.

Benefits:

- **Thymol**: A powerful antimicrobial compound that helps fight infections.
- **Expectorant**: Helps clear mucus from the respiratory tract.

8. Rosemary (Rosmarinus officinalis)

Uses:

- **Cognitive Support**: Rosemary essential oil is believed to enhance memory and concentration.
- **Digestive Health**: Rosemary can aid digestion and relieve bloating.
- **Hair Health**: Applied topically, it may promote hair growth and reduce dandruff.

Benefits:

- **Rosmarinic Acid**: Provides antioxidant and anti-inflammatory benefits.
- **Cognitive Function**: Supports mental clarity and memory.

9. Garlic (Allium sativum)

Uses:

- **Immune Support**: Garlic is known for its ability to boost the immune system and fight infections.

- **Cardiovascular Health**: Helps manage cholesterol levels and support heart health.

- **Antimicrobial**: Effective against bacteria and viruses.

Benefits·

- **Allicin**: A compound with strong antimicrobial and antioxidant properties.

- **Heart Health**: Supports cardiovascular health and reduces blood pressure.

10. Aloe Vera (Aloe barbadensis miller)

Uses:

- **Skin Care**: Aloe vera gel is used to soothe sunburns, minor burns, and skin irritations.

- **Digestive Health**: Aloe vera juice can help with digestive issues and constipation.

Benefits:

- **Polysaccharides**: Help with skin healing and anti-inflammatory effects.

- **Digestive Support**: Aids in digestive health and may help soothe the digestive tract.

How to Store Your Herbs

- **Keep Herbs Dry**: Store dried herbs in airtight containers in a cool, dark place to maintain their potency.

- **Label Containers**: Clearly label containers with the herb name and date to keep track of freshness.

- **Regularly Check for Freshness**: Replace herbs that have lost their aroma or potency.

Having these essential herbs on hand provides a natural and effective way to manage common health issues, enhance your meals, and support overall well-being. From peppermint and chamomile for digestive health to turmeric and garlic for inflammation, each herb offers unique benefits. Ensure proper storage to maintain their efficacy and consult with a healthcare provider for specific health concerns or before starting new herbal remedies.

Tools and Supplies for Making Herbal Remedies

Creating herbal remedies at home can be both fulfilling and cost-effective. To ensure your herbal preparations are safe, effective, and enjoyable to make, you'll need some essential tools and supplies. Here's a guide to the must-have items for crafting your own herbal remedies.

1. Basic Kitchen Tools

1.1. Mortar and Pestle

- **Purpose**: To grind and crush herbs into powders or pastes.

- **Materials**: Typically made from ceramic, stone, or stainless steel.

- **Tip**: Choose a size that suits your needs; a larger one is ideal for grinding bulk herbs, while a smaller one is better for precision tasks.

1.2. Measuring Spoons and Cups

- **Purpose**: To measure herbs and liquids accurately.

- **Materials**: Usually stainless steel or plastic.

- **Tip**: Use dedicated measuring spoons for herbal preparations to avoid contamination from other kitchen uses.

1.3. Strainer or Cheesecloth

- **Purpose**: To filter out solid herb particles from liquids.

- **Materials**: Stainless steel for strainers, and fine-woven cotton or cheesecloth.

- **Tip**: For finer filtering, double or triple layers of cheesecloth work best.

1.4. Mixing Bowls

- **Purpose**: For combining ingredients and making herbal blends.

- **Materials**: Glass, ceramic, or stainless steel.

- **Tip**: Choose non-reactive bowls to avoid any chemical reactions with the herbs.

1.5. Glass Jars and Bottles

- **Purpose**: For storing dried herbs, tinctures, and oils.

- **Materials**: Preferably dark glass to protect contents from light.

- **Tip**: Use airtight jars to maintain freshness and prevent contamination.

2. Herbal Extraction Tools

2.1. Double Boiler

- **Purpose**: To gently heat and infuse herbs into oils or butters without direct heat.

- **Materials**: Stainless steel or heat-resistant glass.

- **Tip**: Ensure the top boiler fits snugly over the bottom one to avoid steam escaping.

2.2. Dropper Bottles

- **Purpose**: For dispensing tinctures and essential oils.

- **Materials**: Glass with a dropper cap.

- **Tip**: Choose amber or cobalt blue bottles to protect sensitive contents from light.

2.3. Pipettes

- **Purpose**: To measure and transfer small amounts of liquid extracts.

- **Materials**: Plastic or glass.

- **Tip**: Use disposable pipettes for convenience and to avoid cross-contamination.

2.4. Herb Grinder or Blender

- **Purpose**: To finely grind herbs or blend them into powders.

- **Materials**: Stainless steel or durable plastic.

- **Tip**: A dedicated herb grinder or high-speed blender can handle various textures and quantities.

3. Preparation and Storage Supplies

3.1. Labels and Markers

- **Purpose**: To label jars, bottles, and other containers with the herb name, date, and type of preparation.

- **Materials**: Waterproof labels and permanent markers.

- **Tip**: Use a label maker for a professional look or handwritten labels for a personal touch.

3.2. Funnels

- **Purpose**: To transfer liquids into bottles or jars without spills.

- **Materials**: Stainless steel or plastic.

- **Tip**: Choose a funnel with a wide mouth for easier transfer and a narrow tip for precision.

3.3. Essential Oil Dilution Kit

- **Purpose**: To safely dilute essential oils for topical use.

- **Materials**: Carrier oils (such as jojoba or fractionated coconut oil) and dilution guidelines.

- **Tip**: Follow recommended dilution ratios to ensure safety and effectiveness.

3.4. Herbal Extraction Equipment

- **Purpose**: To create tinctures and other liquid extracts.

- **Materials**: Equipment like a tincture press or specialized herbal extraction tools.

- **Tip**: Invest in quality extraction tools for efficient and effective herbal extractions.

4. Safety and Hygiene Supplies

4.1. Gloves

- **Purpose**: To maintain hygiene while handling herbs and preparing remedies.

- **Materials**: Disposable latex or nitrile gloves.

- **Tip**: Use gloves to prevent contamination and protect your skin from any irritants.

4.2. Sanitizing Solutions

- **Purpose**: To clean tools and surfaces.

- **Materials**: Rubbing alcohol or a solution of water and vinegar.

- **Tip**: Regularly sanitize tools to maintain a clean workspace and prevent cross-contamination.

4.3. Thermometer

- **Purpose**: To monitor temperatures while heating herbs or creating extracts.

- **Materials**: Digital or glass thermometer.

- **Tip**: Use a thermometer to avoid overheating and ensure proper extraction temperatures.

5. Additional Tools for Advanced Preparations

5.1. Herbal Press

- **Purpose**: To extract juice or essential oils from herbs.

- **Materials**: Metal or wood construction.

- **Tip**: Use for creating potent extracts and oils from fresh herbs.

5.2. Drying Racks

- **Purpose**: To dry herbs thoroughly before storage.
- **Materials**: Mesh or slatted racks.
- **Tip**: Ensure herbs are completely dry before storing to prevent mold growth.

Equipping yourself with these essential tools and supplies can make the process of making herbal remedies smoother and more efficient. From basic kitchen tools like mortar and pestle to specialized equipment for tincture extraction, having the right tools ensures that your herbal preparations are safe, effective, and enjoyable. Invest in quality tools and maintain good hygiene practices to get the most out of your herbal remedy-making endeavors.

Storing and Preserving Your Herbs

Proper storage and preservation are crucial for maintaining the potency, flavor, and effectiveness of your herbs. Whether you're dealing with dried herbs, tinctures, or essential oils, understanding the best practices for storage will help ensure that your herbs remain in optimal condition. Here's a comprehensive guide to storing and preserving your herbs:

1. Storing Dried Herbs

**1.1. Containers

- **Materials**: Use airtight containers made from glass, ceramic, or food-grade plastic.
- **Types**: Mason jars, glass jars with tight-fitting lids, or vacuum-sealed bags.

**1.2. Storage Conditions

- **Light**: Store herbs in dark or opaque containers to protect them from light, which can degrade essential oils and active compounds.
- **Temperature**: Keep herbs in a cool, dry place. Avoid direct sunlight and heat sources that can cause deterioration.
- **Humidity**: Ensure that the storage area is dry. Moisture can lead to mold growth and spoilage.

**1.3. Labeling

- **Details**: Label each container with the herb's name, the date of harvest or purchase, and any relevant information about the herb's use.

- **Tip**: Use waterproof labels or markers to prevent fading.

2. Storing Fresh Herbs

**2.1. Refrigeration

- **Containers**: Store fresh herbs in plastic bags, perforated plastic containers, or lightly wrapped in paper towels.

- **Tips**:
  - **For leafy herbs**: Wrap them in a damp paper towel and place them in a plastic bag.
  - **For stemmed herbs**: Place the stems in a jar with a small amount of water, similar to a bouquet, and cover the top loosely with a plastic bag.

**2.2. Freezing

- **Method**: Wash, chop, and freeze fresh herbs in ice cube trays with a little water or oil. Once frozen, transfer the cubes to freezer bags.

- **Benefits**: Freezing preserves the herbs' flavors and makes them convenient for cooking.

**2.3. Drying

- **Methods**: Air drying, oven drying, or using a food dehydrator.

- **Air Drying**: Tie herb bundles and hang them in a cool, dry, and well-ventilated area.

- **Oven Drying**: Place herbs on a baking sheet and dry at a low temperature (below 180°F or 80°C) with the oven door slightly ajar.

- **Dehydrator**: Follow the manufacturer's instructions for drying herbs.

3. Preserving Herbal Infusions

**3.1. Tinctures

- **Containers**: Store tinctures in dark glass bottles with dropper caps.

- **Conditions**: Keep tinctures in a cool, dark place. Properly sealed, they can last for several years.

**3.2. Herbal Oils

- **Containers**: Use dark glass bottles to protect the oil from light.

- **Conditions**: Store in a cool, dark place. Homemade herbal oils generally last for 6-12 months.

**3.3. Herbal Vinegars

- **Containers**: Store in clean glass bottles or jars.

- **Conditions**: Keep in a cool, dark place. Herbal vinegars can last up to a year if properly sealed.

4. Preserving Herbal Powders and Extracts

**4.1. Herbal Powders

- **Containers**: Use airtight jars or vacuum-sealed bags.

- **Conditions**: Store in a cool, dry place away from light and moisture. Powders generally maintain potency for 6-12 months.

**4.2. Herbal Extracts

- **Containers**: Use dark glass bottles with secure lids.

- **Conditions**: Store in a cool, dark place. Extracts can last for several years if stored properly.

5. General Preservation Tips

**5.1. Avoid Cross-Contamination

- **Practice**: Always use clean, dry utensils when handling herbs to prevent introducing moisture or contaminants.

**5.2. Monitor Freshness

- **Check Regularly**: Periodically check stored herbs for signs of mold, discoloration, or loss of aroma and discard any compromised herbs.

**5.3. Proper Use of Desiccants

- **Desiccants**: Consider using silica gel packets in storage containers to absorb excess moisture and prolong shelf life.

6. Specific Herb Considerations

**6.1. Spices vs. Medicinal Herbs

- **Spices**: Store ground spices in airtight containers away from light and heat; they typically have a shorter shelf life than dried herbs.

- **Medicinal Herbs**: May require specific storage conditions based on their properties and preparation methods.

**6.2. Essential Oils

- **Containers**: Use amber or cobalt blue glass bottles to protect from light.

- **Conditions**: Store in a cool place away from heat sources. Essential oils have a shelf life of 1-3 years depending on the type.

Properly storing and preserving your herbs ensures that they remain potent, flavorful, and effective for use in your remedies. By using airtight containers, keeping herbs away from light and moisture, and labeling them clearly, you can maintain the quality of your herbal preparations and enjoy their benefits for an extended period. Regularly check the condition of your stored herbs and use preservation techniques appropriate for each type of herb and preparation.

DIY Projects: Making Herbal Tinctures, Teas, and Salves

Creating your own herbal remedies can be a rewarding experience, allowing you to tailor treatments to your specific needs and preferences. Below is a comprehensive guide on how to make herbal tinctures, teas, and salves.

1. Making Herbal Tinctures

Herbal tinctures are concentrated extracts of herbs made by soaking them in alcohol or vinegar. They are potent and have a long shelf life, making them a valuable addition to your herbal apothecary.

**1.1. Ingredients and Supplies

- **Herbs**: Fresh or dried herbs.

- **Solvent**: High-proof alcohol (e.g., vodka, brandy) or apple cider vinegar for a non-alcoholic option.

- **Containers**: Glass jars with tight-fitting lids.

- **Strainer or Cheesecloth**: For filtering out herbs.

- **Dropper Bottles**: For storing tinctures.

**1.2. Instructions

1. **Preparation**: Chop fresh herbs or crush dried herbs to increase the surface area for extraction.

2. **Mixing**: Place the herbs in a glass jar and cover them with alcohol or vinegar, making sure the liquid completely covers the herbs.

3. **Infusion**: Seal the jar tightly and store it in a dark, cool place. Shake the jar daily to mix the contents.

4. **Extraction Time**: Let the herbs infuse for 4-6 weeks.

5. **Straining**: After the infusion period, strain the tincture through a cheesecloth or fine strainer into a clean jar or bottle.

6. **Storage**: Transfer the strained tincture into dropper bottles. Store in a cool, dark place.

1.3. **Dosage and Use

- **Dosage**: Typically 1-3 dropperfuls per day, but consult specific dosage guidelines for each herb.

- **Use**: Tinctures can be taken directly, added to water, or incorporated into other preparations.

2. Making Herbal Teas

Herbal teas, also known as infusions or tisanes, are a simple and soothing way to enjoy the benefits of herbs. They can be made using fresh or dried herbs and are great for daily consumption or therapeutic use.

2.1. **Ingredients and Supplies

- **Herbs**: Fresh or dried herbs.

- **Water**: Filtered or spring water.

- **Teapot or Kettle**: For boiling water.

- **Teacup or Strainer**: For steeping the tea.

2.2. **Instructions

1. **Preparation**: If using dried herbs, use about 1-2 teaspoons per cup of water. For fresh herbs, use about 2-4 teaspoons per cup.

2. **Boiling**: Heat water to just below boiling (around 200°F or 93°C) to avoid burning the herbs.

3. **Steeping**: Place the herbs in a teapot or cup and pour hot water over them. Let steep for 5-10 minutes.

4. **Straining**: Strain the herbs out of the tea using a fine-mesh strainer or tea infuser.

5. **Serving**: Enjoy the tea hot or cold. You can sweeten it with honey or lemon if desired.

**2.3. Types of Herbal Teas

- **Infusions**: Made with delicate herbs like mint and chamomile.

- **Decoctions**: Made by simmering tougher plant materials like roots and bark for 15-30 minutes.

3. Making Herbal Salves

Herbal salves are topical preparations used to soothe, heal, and protect the skin. They are often made by infusing herbs into oils and then mixing with a beeswax base.

**3.1. Ingredients and Supplies

- **Herbs**: Fresh or dried herbs.

- **Carrier Oil**: Olive oil, coconut oil, or almond oil.

- **Beeswax**: For thickening the salve.

- **Containers**: Small glass jars or tins.

- **Double Boiler**: For melting the beeswax and oil.

**3.2. Instructions

1. **Infusing Oil**:

   o **Method**: Place herbs in a clean glass jar and cover with carrier oil. Seal the jar and place it in a double boiler or slow cooker on low heat for 2-4 hours. Alternatively, infuse herbs in oil at room temperature for 4-6 weeks, shaking daily.

   o **Strain**: After infusion, strain the oil through cheesecloth or a fine-mesh strainer into a clean bowl or jar.

2. **Making the Salve**:

   o **Melting**: In a double boiler, melt beeswax until it becomes liquid.

   o **Combining**: Add the infused oil to the melted beeswax and stir until well combined.

- Testing Consistency: To test the consistency, place a small amount of the mixture on a cold spoon and let it cool. Adjust the beeswax if needed to achieve the desired firmness.

- Pouring: Pour the salve into clean containers while still warm. Allow it to cool and harden before sealing.

**3.3. Storage and Use

- Storage: Keep salves in a cool, dry place. Properly made salves can last for 6-12 months.

- Use: Apply a thin layer to affected areas as needed.

Making your own herbal tinctures, teas, and salves allows you to harness the power of herbs in a personal and effective way. By following these simple steps, you can create potent and versatile herbal remedies that suit your individual needs. Always use high-quality ingredients, maintain cleanliness throughout the preparation process, and store your remedies properly to ensure their effectiveness and longevity.

The Power of Prevention: Using Herbs for Long-Term Wellness

Building Immunity with Herbal Tonics

Herbal tonics have been used for centuries to enhance the immune system and protect against diseases. These natural remedies combine various herbs known for their immune-boosting properties, providing a gentle yet effective way to support your body's defenses. In this section, we will explore key herbs that contribute to immune health and offer practical recipes for incorporating these powerful plants into your daily routine.

Key Herbs for Immune-Boosting Tonics

1. **Echinacea**:

   o **Benefits**: Echinacea is known for its ability to enhance the immune system, particularly by increasing the production of white blood cells. It is effective in preventing and reducing the duration of colds and flu.

   o **Usage**: Commonly used in teas, tinctures, and capsules.

2. **Astragalus**:

   o **Benefits**: Astragalus strengthens the immune system, combats stress, and increases the body's resistance to infections. It also supports overall vitality and energy levels.

   o **Usage**: Often used in soups, teas, and tinctures.

3. **Elderberry**:

   o **Benefits**: Elderberry is rich in antioxidants and vitamins that boost the immune system. It is particularly effective in preventing and alleviating cold and flu symptoms.

   o **Usage**: Commonly used in syrups, teas, and gummies.

4. **Ginger**:

   o **Benefits**: Ginger has powerful anti-inflammatory and antioxidant properties. It helps in enhancing the immune response and relieving respiratory issues.

   o **Usage**: Used fresh, dried, or in teas and tinctures.

5. **Turmeric**:

   o **Benefits**: Turmeric contains curcumin, which has strong anti-inflammatory and antioxidant effects. It supports the immune system and helps in fighting off infections.

   o **Usage**: Commonly used in teas, golden milk, and as a spice in cooking.

Recipes for Immune-Boosting Tonics

Echinacea Immune-Boosting Tea

- **Ingredients**:

   o 1 teaspoon dried Echinacea root

   o 1 teaspoon dried elderberries

   o 1 teaspoon dried astragalus root

   o 2 cups of water

   o Honey to taste

   o Lemon juice (optional)

- **Instructions**:

1. Combine the dried herbs in a small pot.

2. Add water and bring to a boil.

3. Reduce heat and let it simmer for 20 minutes.

4. Strain the tea into a cup.

5. Add honey and lemon juice to taste.

6. Enjoy a cup daily to boost your immune system.

Astragalus and Ginger Tonic

- **Ingredients**:

   o 1 tablespoon dried astragalus root

   o 1 tablespoon fresh ginger, sliced

   o 3 cups of water

   o 1 teaspoon honey (optional)

- **Instructions**:
1. Place the astragalus root and ginger slices in a saucepan.
2. Add water and bring to a boil.
3. Reduce heat and simmer for 30 minutes.
4. Strain the tonic into a jar.
5. Add honey if desired and stir well.
6. Drink a cup daily for immune support.

Elderberry Syrup

- **Ingredients**:
  - 1 cup fresh or dried elderberries
  - 3 cups of water
  - 1 cup raw honey
  - 1 teaspoon cinnamon powder
  - 1 teaspoon ground ginger
  - 1/2 teaspoon ground cloves

- **Instructions**:
1. Combine elderberries and water in a saucepan.
2. Bring to a boil, then reduce heat and simmer for 45 minutes.
3. Mash the berries and strain the liquid into a bowl.
4. Add honey, cinnamon, ginger, and cloves to the liquid and stir well.
5. Pour the syrup into a glass jar and store it in the refrigerator.
6. Take one tablespoon daily for immune support.

Conclusion

Incorporating herbal tonics into your daily routine is a simple and effective way to boost your immune system and protect against illnesses. By using herbs like Echinacea, astragalus, elderberry, ginger, and turmeric, you can create powerful natural remedies that support your body's defenses and promote overall wellness. Start experimenting with these recipes and discover the benefits of herbal immunity boosters.

Detoxifying Your Body Naturally

Detoxification is the process of removing toxins and impurities from the body to improve overall health and well-being. While the body has its own mechanisms for detoxification, certain herbs can enhance and support these processes. This section explores key herbs that aid in natural detoxification and provides practical recipes to incorporate them into your routine.

Key Herbs for Detoxification

1. **Milk Thistle**:

   o **Benefits**: Milk thistle is renowned for its liver-protective properties. It contains silymarin, which helps regenerate liver cells, detoxify harmful substances, and protect the liver from damage.

   o **Usage**: Often used in teas, tinctures, and capsules.

2. **Dandelion Root**:

   o **Benefits**: Dandelion root supports liver and kidney function, promoting the elimination of toxins. It also aids in digestion and acts as a natural diuretic, helping to flush out excess fluids.

   o **Usage**: Commonly used in teas, tinctures, and as a coffee substitute.

3. **Burdock Root**:

   o **Benefits**: Burdock root is a powerful blood purifier. It helps detoxify the liver and kidneys and is beneficial for skin health. It also has anti-inflammatory and antioxidant properties.

   o **Usage**: Used in teas, tinctures, and as a culinary ingredient in soups and stews.

4. **Turmeric**:

   o **Benefits**: Turmeric supports liver detoxification and has strong anti-inflammatory and antioxidant effects. It helps protect the liver from damage and supports overall liver health.

   o **Usage**: Commonly used in teas, golden milk, and as a spice in cooking.

5. **Ginger**:

- **Benefits**: Ginger aids digestion, reduces inflammation, and supports detoxification processes. It helps stimulate circulation and sweating, which can aid in the elimination of toxins.
- **Usage**: Used fresh, dried, or in teas and tinctures.

Recipes for Detoxifying Remedies

Milk Thistle Liver Detox Tea

- **Ingredients**:
    - 1 teaspoon dried milk thistle seeds
    - 1 teaspoon dried dandelion root
    - 1 teaspoon dried burdock root
    - 2 cups of water
    - Lemon juice (optional)
    - Honey to taste

- **Instructions**:
1. Combine the dried herbs in a small pot.
2. Add water and bring to a boil.
3. Reduce heat and let it simmer for 20 minutes.
4. Strain the tea into a cup.
5. Add lemon juice and honey to taste.
6. Drink a cup daily to support liver detoxification.

Dandelion Root Coffee Substitute

- **Ingredients**:
    - 1 tablespoon roasted dandelion root
    - 1 cup of water
    - Almond milk (optional)
    - Sweetener of choice (optional)

- **Instructions**:

1. Place the roasted dandelion root in a pot.

2. Add water and bring to a boil.

3. Reduce heat and let it simmer for 10 minutes.

4. Strain into a cup.

5. Add almond milk and sweetener if desired.

6. Enjoy as a coffee alternative that supports liver detoxification.

Burdock and Ginger Detox Elixir

- **Ingredients**:
    - 1 tablespoon fresh burdock root, sliced
    - 1 tablespoon fresh ginger, sliced
    - 2 cups of water
    - 1 tablespoon lemon juice
    - 1 teaspoon honey

- **Instructions**:

1. Place the burdock root and ginger slices in a saucepan.

2. Add water and bring to a boil.

3. Reduce heat and simmer for 20 minutes.

4. Strain the elixir into a jar.

5. Add lemon juice and honey, stirring well.

6. Drink a cup daily for detoxification support.

Conclusion

Detoxifying your body naturally with herbs is an effective way to enhance your health and vitality. Herbs like milk thistle, dandelion root, burdock root, turmeric, and ginger offer powerful detoxification benefits, supporting the liver, kidneys, and overall detox processes. By incorporating these herbs into your daily routine through teas, elixirs, and other preparations, you can promote the elimination of toxins and achieve a greater sense of well-being.

Supporting Heart Health with Herbs

Heart health is essential for overall well-being, and incorporating heart-supportive herbs into your daily routine can be an effective way to maintain cardiovascular function and prevent heart disease. This section explores key herbs known for their heart health benefits and provides practical recipes for integrating these powerful plants into your lifestyle.

Key Herbs for Heart Health

1. **Hawthorn**:

    o **Benefits**: Hawthorn is renowned for its cardiovascular benefits, including improving heart function, reducing blood pressure, and supporting healthy circulation. It strengthens the heart muscle and helps manage symptoms of heart failure.

    o **Usage**: Commonly used in teas, tinctures, and capsules.

2. **Garlic**:

    o **Benefits**: Garlic has been shown to reduce blood pressure, lower cholesterol levels, and prevent atherosclerosis (hardening of the arteries). It also has anti-inflammatory and antioxidant properties.

    o **Usage**: Used fresh, in capsules, or as an ingredient in cooking.

3. **Turmeric**:

    o **Benefits**: Turmeric supports heart health by reducing inflammation, improving blood flow, and preventing blood clots. Its active compound, curcumin, has powerful antioxidant effects that protect the heart.

    o **Usage**: Commonly used in teas, golden milk, and as a spice in cooking.

4. **Cayenne Pepper**:

    o **Benefits**: Cayenne pepper improves circulation, lowers blood pressure, and reduces cholesterol levels. It also helps to strengthen the heart and improve overall cardiovascular function.

    o **Usage**: Used in teas, tinctures, or as a spice in cooking.

5. **Motherwort**:

- **Benefits**: Motherwort is known for its ability to calm the nervous system and reduce stress, which can benefit heart health. It also helps to regulate heartbeat and improve overall cardiovascular function.
- **Usage**: Often used in teas and tinctures.

Recipes for Heart-Healthy Remedies

Hawthorn Heart Health Tea

- **Ingredients**:
    - 1 teaspoon dried hawthorn berries
    - 1 teaspoon dried hawthorn leaves and flowers
    - 2 cups of water
    - Honey to taste (optional)
    - Lemon slice (optional)

- **Instructions**:

1. Combine the dried hawthorn berries, leaves, and flowers in a small pot.
2. Add water and bring to a boil.
3. Reduce heat and let it simmer for 15-20 minutes.
4. Strain the tea into a cup.
5. Add honey and a lemon slice if desired.
6. Drink a cup daily to support heart health.

Garlic and Turmeric Heart Health Tonic

- **Ingredients**:
    - 1 clove garlic, minced
    - 1 teaspoon fresh turmeric root, grated (or 1/2 teaspoon ground turmeric)
    - 1 cup of warm water
    - 1 tablespoon lemon juice
    - 1 teaspoon honey (optional)

- **Instructions**:

1. Combine the minced garlic and grated turmeric in a cup.

2. Add warm water and let it steep for 5-10 minutes.

3. Add lemon juice and honey, stirring well.

4. Drink daily for heart health benefits.

Cayenne and Lemon Circulation Boost Drink

- **Ingredients**:
    - 1/4 teaspoon cayenne pepper
    - 1 tablespoon lemon juice
    - 1 cup of warm water
    - 1 teaspoon honey (optional)

- **Instructions**:

1. Mix the cayenne pepper and lemon juice in a cup.

2. Add warm water and stir well.

3. Add honey if desired.

4. Drink this mixture once daily to improve circulation and support heart health.

Motherwort Calming Heart Tea

- **Ingredients**:
    - 1 teaspoon dried motherwort
    - 1 teaspoon dried lemon balm (optional)
    - 1 cup of boiling water
    - Honey to taste (optional)

- **Instructions**:

1. Place the dried motherwort and lemon balm in a cup.

2. Pour boiling water over the herbs.

3. Let it steep for 10-15 minutes.

4. Strain the tea into another cup.

5. Add honey if desired.

6.   Drink daily to support heart health and reduce stress.

Conclusion

Using herbs to support heart health is a natural and effective way to maintain cardiovascular function and prevent heart disease. By incorporating herbs like hawthorn, garlic, turmeric, cayenne pepper, and motherwort into your daily routine, you can promote healthy heart function, improve circulation, and reduce the risk of cardiovascular issues. Start experimenting with these recipes and discover the heart-healthy benefits of herbal remedies.

Maintaining Healthy Blood Sugar Levels

Maintaining healthy blood sugar levels is crucial for overall health and well-being. Unstable blood sugar levels can lead to conditions such as diabetes, metabolic syndrome, and other health complications. Incorporating certain herbs into your daily routine can help regulate blood sugar levels naturally. This section explores key herbs known for their blood sugar-balancing properties and provides practical recipes for integrating them into your lifestyle.

Key Herbs for Blood Sugar Regulation

1. **Cinnamon**:

   o **Benefits**: Cinnamon is well-known for its ability to improve insulin sensitivity and lower blood sugar levels. It helps slow the breakdown of carbohydrates in the digestive tract, leading to a more gradual release of glucose into the bloodstream.

   o **Usage**: Commonly used in teas, smoothies, and as a spice in cooking and baking.

2. **Fenugreek**:

   o **Benefits**: Fenugreek seeds contain soluble fiber, which helps regulate blood sugar levels by slowing down carbohydrate absorption. They also help improve insulin function and reduce fasting blood sugar levels.

   o **Usage**: Used in teas, soaked in water, or as a spice in cooking.

3. **Bitter Melon**:

   o **Benefits**: Bitter melon contains compounds that mimic insulin and help lower blood glucose levels. It also improves glucose utilization by the cells and reduces sugar absorption in the intestines.

- o **Usage**: Used in teas, juices, and as a vegetable in cooking.

4. **Gymnema Sylvestre**:

   - o **Benefits**: Gymnema Sylvestre helps reduce sugar absorption in the intestines and improves insulin function. It also has the unique property of reducing sugar cravings by blocking the taste of sweetness.

   - o **Usage**: Often used in teas, capsules, and tinctures.

5. **Berberine**:

   - o **Benefits**: Berberine is a compound found in several herbs, including goldenseal and barberry. It helps lower blood sugar levels by increasing insulin sensitivity and reducing glucose production in the liver.

   - o **Usage**: Commonly used in capsule or tincture form.

Recipes for Blood Sugar Regulation

Cinnamon Blood Sugar Balancing Tea

- **Ingredients**:

  - o 1 cinnamon stick or 1 teaspoon ground cinnamon

  - o 2 cups of water

  - o 1 teaspoon honey (optional)

  - o Lemon slice (optional)

- **Instructions**:

1. Place the cinnamon stick or ground cinnamon in a pot.

2. Add water and bring to a boil.

3. Reduce heat and let it simmer for 10 minutes.

4. Strain the tea into a cup.

5. Add honey and a lemon slice if desired.

6. Drink a cup daily to help regulate blood sugar levels.

Fenugreek Seed Water

- **Ingredients**:

  - o 1 tablespoon fenugreek seeds

- o   1 cup of water
- **Instructions**:

1. Soak the fenugreek seeds in water overnight.

2. In the morning, strain the seeds and drink the water on an empty stomach.

3. Repeat daily for blood sugar benefits.

Bitter Melon Juice

- **Ingredients**:
  - o   1 medium-sized bitter melon
  - o   1 cup of water
  - o   Lemon juice to taste (optional)
- **Instructions**:

1. Wash the bitter melon thoroughly and remove the seeds.

2. Chop the bitter melon into small pieces.

3. Blend the bitter melon pieces with water until smooth.

4. Strain the juice into a glass.

5. Add lemon juice to taste if desired.

6. Drink once daily to help lower blood sugar levels.

Gymnema Sylvestre Tea

- **Ingredients**:
  - o   1 teaspoon dried Gymnema Sylvestre leaves
  - o   1 cup of boiling water
- **Instructions**:

1. Place the dried Gymnema Sylvestre leaves in a cup.

2. Pour boiling water over the leaves.

3. Let it steep for 5-10 minutes.

4. Strain the tea into another cup.

5. Drink once or twice daily to support blood sugar regulation.

Berberine Supplement

- **Usage Instructions**:
    1. Follow the dosage instructions on the berberine supplement packaging, typically 500 mg taken two to three times daily with meals.
    2. Consult with a healthcare professional before starting any new supplement regimen.

Conclusion

Using herbs to maintain healthy blood sugar levels is a natural and effective way to support your overall health. Herbs like cinnamon, fenugreek, bitter melon, Gymnema Sylvestre, and berberine offer powerful blood sugar-regulating benefits. By incorporating these herbs into your daily routine through teas, tonics, and supplements, you can achieve better blood sugar control and enhance your overall well-being.

Herbs for Longevity and Vitality

Longevity and vitality are essential for maintaining a high quality of life as we age. Herbs can play a significant role in promoting longevity by supporting the body's natural defenses, improving energy levels, and enhancing overall health. This section explores key herbs known for their longevity and vitality benefits and provides practical recipes for integrating them into your daily routine.

Key Herbs for Longevity and Vitality

1. **Ginseng**:
    - **Benefits**: Ginseng is known for its ability to boost energy, improve mental clarity, and enhance physical stamina. It also supports the immune system and helps the body adapt to stress.
    - **Usage**: Commonly used in teas, tinctures, and supplements.

2. **Ashwagandha**:
    - **Benefits**: Ashwagandha is an adaptogenic herb that helps the body manage stress, improve energy levels, and enhance cognitive function. It also supports hormonal balance and boosts the immune system.
    - **Usage**: Used in teas, capsules, and powders.

3. **Reishi Mushroom**:

- o **Benefits**: Reishi mushroom is renowned for its immune-boosting properties, ability to reduce stress, and support for overall longevity. It also has antioxidant effects that protect against cellular damage.
  - o **Usage**: Used in teas, tinctures, and powders.

4. **Turmeric**:
   - o **Benefits**: Turmeric has powerful anti-inflammatory and antioxidant properties that help protect against age-related diseases. It supports joint health, boosts the immune system, and enhances overall vitality.
   - o **Usage**: Commonly used in teas, golden milk, and as a spice in cooking.

5. **Astragalus**:
   - o **Benefits**: Astragalus is known for its immune-boosting and anti-aging properties. It helps protect against cellular damage, supports heart health, and enhances energy levels.
   - o **Usage**: Used in teas, tinctures, and supplements.

Recipes for Longevity and Vitality

Ginseng Vitality Tea

- **Ingredients**:
  - o 1 teaspoon dried ginseng root slices
  - o 2 cups of water
  - o Honey to taste (optional)
  - o Lemon slice (optional)

- **Instructions**:

1. Place the dried ginseng root slices in a small pot.
2. Add water and bring to a boil.
3. Reduce heat and let it simmer for 20-30 minutes.
4. Strain the tea into a cup.
5. Add honey and a lemon slice if desired.
6. Drink a cup daily to boost energy and vitality.

Ashwagandha Stress Relief Latte

- **Ingredients**:
    - 1 teaspoon ashwagandha powder
    - 1 cup of milk (dairy or plant-based)
    - 1/2 teaspoon cinnamon powder
    - 1/2 teaspoon turmeric powder
    - 1 teaspoon honey or maple syrup
- **Instructions**:

1. Heat the milk in a small saucepan over medium heat.

2. Add ashwagandha, cinnamon, and turmeric powders to the milk.

3. Stir well until the powders are fully dissolved.

4. Remove from heat and add honey or maple syrup.

5. Pour into a cup and enjoy daily to support stress management and vitality.

Reishi Mushroom Immune Boosting Tea

- **Ingredients**:
    - 1 teaspoon dried reishi mushroom slices or powder
    - 2 cups of water
    - Honey to taste (optional)
    - Ginger slice (optional)
- **Instructions**:

1. Place the dried reishi mushroom slices or powder in a small pot.

2. Add water and bring to a boil.

3. Reduce heat and let it simmer for 20-30 minutes.

4. Strain the tea into a cup.

5. Add honey and a ginger slice if desired.

6. Drink a cup daily to boost immunity and promote longevity.

Golden Milk for Anti-Inflammatory Benefits

- **Ingredients**:

- o   1 cup of milk (dairy or plant-based)

- o   1 teaspoon turmeric powder

- o   1/2 teaspoon cinnamon powder

- o   1/4 teaspoon ginger powder

- o   1 teaspoon honey or maple syrup

- o   A pinch of black pepper

- **Instructions**:

1.   Heat the milk in a small saucepan over medium heat.

2.   Add turmeric, cinnamon, ginger powders, and a pinch of black pepper to the milk.

3.   Stir well until the spices are fully dissolved.

4.   Remove from heat and add honey or maple syrup.

5.   Pour into a cup and enjoy daily for anti-inflammatory benefits and overall vitality.

Astragalus Longevity Tonic

- **Ingredients**:

- o   1 tablespoon dried astragalus root

- o   2 cups of water

- o   Honey to taste (optional)

- o   Lemon slice (optional)

- **Instructions**:

1.   Place the dried astragalus root in a small pot.

2.   Add water and bring to a boil.

3.   Reduce heat and let it simmer for 30-40 minutes.

4.   Strain the tonic into a cup.

5.   Add honey and a lemon slice if desired.

6.   Drink a cup daily to support longevity and energy levels.

Conclusion

Incorporating herbs that promote longevity and vitality into your daily routine is a natural and effective way to enhance overall health and well-being. Herbs like ginseng, ashwagandha, reishi mushroom, turmeric, and astragalus offer powerful benefits that can help you maintain energy levels, boost immunity, and protect against age-related diseases. Start experimenting with these recipes and discover the long-lasting benefits of herbal remedies for longevity and vitality.

Integrating Natural Remedies into Daily Life

Incorporating Herbs into Your Diet

Incorporating herbs into your diet is a delicious and effective way to enhance your overall health and well-being. Herbs not only add flavor and variety to your meals but also offer numerous health benefits, from boosting immunity to aiding digestion. This section provides practical tips and recipes for integrating herbs into your daily diet.

Herbal Teas

Benefits: Herbal teas are an easy way to enjoy the health benefits of herbs. They can support various health needs, such as relaxation, digestion, and detoxification.

How to Use:

- Brew a cup of herbal tea daily to support specific health needs. For example, chamomile tea can aid in relaxation and sleep, while peppermint tea can help with digestion.

- Experiment with blending different herbs to create your own tea blends tailored to your preferences.

Example Recipe: Chamomile Mint Tea

- **Ingredients**:
    - 1 tablespoon dried chamomile flowers
    - 1 teaspoon dried mint leaves
    - 2 cups boiling water
    - Honey (optional)

- **Instructions**:

1. Combine chamomile and mint in a teapot or heatproof container.

2. Pour boiling water over the herbs.

3. Steep for 5-7 minutes, then strain.

4. Sweeten with honey if desired.

Herb-Infused Cooking

Benefits: Adding herbs to your cooking enhances flavor and provides a boost of nutrients and antioxidants.

How to Use:

- Incorporate fresh or dried herbs into dishes like soups, stews, salads, and roasted vegetables.
- Use herbs in homemade sauces, dressings, and marinades to add flavor without extra calories or sodium.

Example Recipe: **Herb-Infused Roasted Vegetables**

- **Ingredients**:
  - 4 cups mixed vegetables (e.g., bell peppers, zucchini, carrots)
  - 2 tablespoons olive oil
  - 1 tablespoon fresh rosemary, chopped
  - 1 tablespoon fresh thyme, chopped
  - Salt and pepper to taste
- **Instructions**:
1. Preheat the oven to 400°F (200°C).
2. Toss vegetables with olive oil, rosemary, thyme, salt, and pepper.
3. Spread vegetables on a baking sheet.
4. Roast for 20-25 minutes or until tender and golden brown.

Smoothies and Juices

Benefits: Adding herbs to smoothies and juices increases their nutritional value and offers specific health benefits.

How to Use:

- Blend herbs like spinach, kale, mint, and parsley into your favorite smoothies and juices.
- Combine herbs with fruits and vegetables for a nutrient-rich drink that supports overall health.

Example Recipe: **Green Herb Smoothie**

- **Ingredients**:
    - 1 cup spinach
    - 1/2 cup parsley
    - 1 banana
    - 1/2 cup frozen mango
    - 1 cup almond milk or other plant-based milk
- **Instructions**:
1. Combine all ingredients in a blender.
2. Blend until smooth.
3. Serve immediately.

Herbal Supplements

Benefits: Herbal supplements offer a concentrated dose of beneficial herbs and can support various health needs.

How to Use:

- Choose supplements that align with your health goals, such as turmeric capsules for inflammation or echinacea for immune support.
- Follow the recommended dosage on the product label and consult with a healthcare professional if you have any concerns.

Example: **Turmeric Capsules**

- **Usage**: Take as directed, usually 1-2 capsules per day, to support joint health and reduce inflammation.

Tips for Incorporating Herbs into Your Diet

1. **Start Small**: Begin by adding a few herbs to your meals and gradually increase their use as you become more accustomed to their flavors and benefits.
2. **Grow Your Own**: Growing herbs in your garden or on your windowsill ensures a fresh supply and encourages regular use.
3. **Experiment with Recipes**: Try new recipes and cooking techniques to discover different ways to enjoy herbs in your diet.

4. **Combine Herbs**: Mix herbs to create unique flavors and health benefits. For example, combine basil and oregano for a Mediterranean-inspired dish or cilantro and lime for a fresh, zesty flavor.

Conclusion

Incorporating herbs into your diet is a simple and enjoyable way to enhance your health and add variety to your meals. Whether through herbal teas, cooking, smoothies, or supplements, herbs offer numerous benefits that can support your well-being. Start integrating herbs into your daily routine and enjoy the delicious and health-promoting results.

Herbal Bath and Body Care: Recipes for Natural Beauty

Herbal bath and body care offers a natural and effective way to enhance your beauty routine while benefiting from the healing properties of herbs. From soothing baths to nourishing skincare, incorporating herbs into your personal care regimen can support your skin health, relaxation, and overall well-being. This section explores various herbal bath and body care recipes to help you create your own natural beauty products at home.

Herbal Baths

Benefits: Herbal baths can relax your muscles, soothe your skin, and provide aromatherapy benefits. They are a great way to unwind and pamper yourself after a long day.

How to Use:

- Add herbal bath products to your bathwater to enjoy the therapeutic benefits.

- Experiment with different herb combinations to create your ideal bath experience.

Example Recipe: Relaxing Lavender Chamomile Bath

- **Ingredients**:
    - 1 cup dried lavender flowers
    - 1 cup dried chamomile flowers
    - 1/2 cup Epsom salt
    - 1/4 cup baking soda
    - 1 tablespoon dried rose petals (optional)

- **Instructions**:

1. Combine lavender, chamomile, Epsom salt, baking soda, and rose petals in a bowl.

2. Place the mixture in a muslin bag or cheesecloth and tie it closed.

3. Drop the bag into your bathwater and let it steep for 10-15 minutes before getting in.

4. Relax and enjoy the soothing effects.

Herbal Skincare

Benefits: Herbal skincare products can help address specific skin concerns, such as acne, dryness, and inflammation, while providing nourishment and hydration.

How to Use:

- Apply herbal skincare products directly to the skin as directed.

- Use regularly for best results and to maintain healthy, glowing skin.

Example Recipe: **Soothing Calendula Face Mask**

- **Ingredients**:
  - 1 tablespoon dried calendula flowers
  - 1 tablespoon plain yogurt
  - 1 teaspoon honey

- **Instructions**:

1. Crush the dried calendula flowers into a fine powder using a mortar and pestle or spice grinder.

2. Mix the calendula powder with yogurt and honey to form a smooth paste.

3. Apply the mask to your face and leave it on for 15-20 minutes.

4. Rinse off with warm water and pat your face dry.

Example Recipe: **Nourishing Aloe Vera and Green Tea Toner**

- **Ingredients**:
  - 1/2 cup aloe vera juice
  - 1/4 cup brewed green tea, cooled
  - 1 tablespoon witch hazel

- 1 teaspoon rosewater (optional)

- **Instructions**:

1. Mix aloe vera juice, green tea, witch hazel, and rosewater in a bottle.

2. Shake well before each use.

3. Apply to your face with a cotton pad after cleansing.

Herbal Hair Care

Benefits: Herbal hair care products can strengthen hair, promote growth, and improve scalp health. They can also add shine and manageability to your hair.

How to Use:

- Apply herbal hair care products to your hair and scalp as directed.

- Use regularly to support healthy hair and scalp.

Example Recipe: Revitalizing Rosemary Mint Hair Rinse

- **Ingredients**:

  - 1 cup water

  - 1 tablespoon dried rosemary

  - 1 tablespoon dried mint leaves

- **Instructions**:

1. Boil water and pour it over rosemary and mint in a heatproof container.

2. Let the herbs steep for 15-20 minutes, then strain.

3. After shampooing, pour the herbal rinse over your hair and massage into the scalp.

4. Rinse with cool water.

Herbal Body Care

Benefits: Herbal body care products can enhance your daily routine by providing moisturizing and soothing effects, while also offering natural fragrance.

How to Use:

- Apply herbal body care products to clean, dry skin as needed.

- Use regularly to maintain soft, healthy skin.

Example Recipe: **Herbal Body Scrub**

- **Ingredients**:
    - 1 cup sugar (white or brown)
    - 1/2 cup coconut oil
    - 1 tablespoon dried lavender or chamomile flowers
    - 5-10 drops essential oil (e.g., lavender, chamomile, or eucalyptus)

- **Instructions**:

1. Combine sugar and coconut oil in a bowl.
2. Mix in dried herbs and essential oil.
3. Massage the scrub onto damp skin in circular motions, then rinse with warm water.
4. Store any leftover scrub in an airtight container.

Example Recipe: **Herbal Bath Salts**

- **Ingredients**:
    - 1 cup Epsom salt
    - 1/2 cup sea salt
    - 1/4 cup baking soda
    - 1/4 cup dried rose petals
    - 1/4 cup dried lavender flowers
    - 10 drops essential oil (e.g., rose, lavender, or geranium)

- **Instructions**:

1. Combine Epsom salt, sea salt, and baking soda in a bowl.
2. Stir in dried rose petals and lavender flowers.
3. Add essential oil and mix well.
4. Store in a jar and use 1/2 cup per bath.

Conclusion

Incorporating herbs into your bath and body care routine can enhance your natural beauty while providing therapeutic benefits. From relaxing baths to nourishing skincare and hair care, these herbal recipes offer a range of options to help you look and feel your best. Experiment with these recipes and enjoy the natural, soothing effects of herbal remedies in your daily self-care routine.

Using Herbs in Household Cleaning

Using herbs in household cleaning is a natural, effective way to maintain a clean and healthy home environment. Herbs offer antimicrobial, antifungal, and deodorizing properties, making them excellent additions to your cleaning routine. This section explores various ways to incorporate herbs into your household cleaning practices, including recipes for homemade cleaning solutions and tips for using herbs effectively.

Herbal Cleaning Solutions

Benefits: Herbal cleaning solutions are eco-friendly, non-toxic, and often more affordable than commercial cleaners. They can also leave a pleasant natural fragrance while providing effective cleaning power.

How to Use:

- Use herbal cleaning solutions in place of or in conjunction with your regular cleaning products.
- Store homemade cleaners in labeled spray bottles or jars for convenience.

Example Recipe: **Herbal All-Purpose Cleaner**

- **Ingredients**:
    o 1 cup water
    o 1/2 cup white vinegar
    o 1/4 cup baking soda
    o 10 drops essential oil (e.g., tea tree, lavender, or lemon)
- **Instructions**:
1. Mix water, vinegar, and baking soda in a spray bottle.
2. Add essential oil and shake well.
3. Spray onto surfaces and wipe clean with a cloth.
4. Use for general cleaning of countertops, sinks, and other surfaces.

Example Recipe: Citrus Herb Disinfectant

- **Ingredients**:
    - 1 cup water
    - 1/4 cup lemon juice
    - 1/4 cup witch hazel
    - 10 drops essential oil (e.g., lemon, eucalyptus, or rosemary)

- **Instructions**:

1. Combine water, lemon juice, and witch hazel in a spray bottle.

2. Add essential oil and shake well.

3. Spray onto surfaces and wipe with a clean cloth.

4. Ideal for disinfecting kitchen surfaces and bathroom fixtures.

Example Recipe: Minty Glass Cleaner

- **Ingredients**:
    - 1 cup water
    - 1/4 cup white vinegar
    - 1 tablespoon cornstarch
    - 5-10 drops peppermint essential oil

- **Instructions**:

1. Mix water, vinegar, and cornstarch in a spray bottle.

2. Add peppermint essential oil and shake well.

3. Spray onto glass and mirrors, then wipe with a clean, dry cloth for a streak-free shine.

Herbal Air Fresheners

Benefits: Herbal air fresheners can help purify the air and provide a natural, pleasant fragrance without the use of synthetic chemicals.

How to Use:

- Use herbal air fresheners to eliminate odors and add a refreshing scent to your home.

- Place air fresheners in areas prone to odors or use as needed.

Example Recipe: Herbal Room Spray

- **Ingredients**:
  - 1 cup water
  - 2 tablespoons vodka or rubbing alcohol
  - 10 drops essential oil (e.g., lavender, eucalyptus, or citrus)

- **Instructions**:

1. Combine water and vodka in a spray bottle.

2. Add essential oil and shake well.

3. Spray around the room to freshen the air and neutralize odors.

Example Recipe: Herbal Sachets

- **Ingredients**:
  - 1/2 cup dried lavender flowers
  - 1/2 cup dried rosemary leaves
  - 1/4 cup dried rose petals
  - 10 drops essential oil (e.g., lavender or rosemary)

- **Instructions**:

1. Mix dried herbs and essential oil in a bowl.

2. Place the mixture into small fabric sachets or pouches.

3. Place sachets in drawers, closets, or other areas to add a fresh, natural scent.

Herbal Laundry Solutions

Benefits: Herbal laundry solutions can help naturally deodorize and soften fabrics, as well as provide a subtle herbal scent.

How to Use:

- Add herbal laundry solutions to your regular laundry routine for a fresh, clean smell.

- Store homemade laundry products in labeled containers for easy use.

Example Recipe: Herbal Laundry Detergent

- **Ingredients**:
    - 1 cup washing soda
    - 1 cup borax
    - 1 bar of natural soap (grated)
    - 1/4 cup dried lavender flowers
- **Instructions**:
1. Mix washing soda, borax, and grated soap in a bowl.
2. Stir in dried lavender flowers.
3. Use 2 tablespoons of the mixture per load of laundry.

Example Recipe: Herbal Fabric Softener

- **Ingredients**:
    - 1 cup white vinegar
    - 1/2 cup baking soda
    - 10 drops essential oil (e.g., lavender or eucalyptus)
- **Instructions**:
1. Combine vinegar and baking soda in a bowl.
2. Add essential oil and stir to mix.
3. Add to the rinse cycle of your washing machine.

Growing and Using Herbs for Cleaning

Benefits: Growing your own herbs for cleaning ensures a fresh supply and allows you to customize your cleaning products.

How to Use:

- Grow herbs such as lavender, mint, rosemary, and thyme in your garden or indoors.
- Harvest and dry herbs for use in cleaning solutions, air fresheners, and sachets.

Example: Growing and Using Lavender

- **Benefits**: Lavender has antimicrobial properties and a pleasant scent, making it ideal for cleaning and air freshening.

- **How to Use**: Grow lavender in a sunny spot. Harvest flowers when they are in full bloom and dry them for use in sachets or as an ingredient in cleaning solutions.

Conclusion

Using herbs in household cleaning is a natural and effective way to maintain a healthy home environment while benefiting from their aromatic and antimicrobial properties. From herbal cleaning solutions to air fresheners and laundry products, these recipes offer practical and eco-friendly alternatives to conventional cleaning products. Start incorporating herbs into your cleaning routine and enjoy a fresher, more natural home.

Growing Your Own Medicinal Herb Garden

Growing your own medicinal herb garden is a rewarding way to have fresh, natural remedies at your fingertips. Medicinal herbs offer a range of therapeutic benefits, and cultivating your own garden ensures you have a reliable supply of high-quality herbs for health and wellness purposes. This section will guide you through the essentials of starting and maintaining a medicinal herb garden, including selecting herbs, planting, and caring for your garden.

Planning Your Medicinal Herb Garden

Benefits: A well-planned medicinal herb garden allows you to customize your plant selections based on your health needs, local climate, and available space. It also offers the satisfaction of growing your own remedies and the opportunity to connect with nature.

How to Plan:

- **Assess Your Space**: Determine the size and location of your garden, considering sunlight, soil type, and access to water.
- **Choose Herbs**: Select herbs based on their medicinal properties, growing requirements, and your personal health goals. Consider starting with a few versatile herbs and expanding as you gain experience.

Example Herbs to Consider:

- **Lavender**: Calming, helps with sleep and anxiety.
- **Chamomile**: Soothes digestive issues and promotes relaxation.
- **Peppermint**: Aids digestion and relieves headaches.
- **Echinacea**: Boosts the immune system and helps fight colds.

- **Calendula**: Supports skin health and wound healing.

Starting Your Medicinal Herb Garden

Benefits: Starting your garden from seeds or seedlings gives you control over the quality and growth of your plants. It also allows you to experience the full lifecycle of the herbs.

How to Start:

- **Gather Supplies**: Purchase seeds or seedlings, soil, pots (if starting indoors), and gardening tools.

- **Prepare the Soil**: Use well-draining soil rich in organic matter. If planting in containers, use potting mix suitable for herbs.

- **Planting**:

  o **Seeds**: Follow the instructions on seed packets for depth and spacing. Generally, seeds are sown 1/4 to 1/2 inch deep.

  o **Seedlings**: Plant seedlings at the same depth they were in their nursery pots. Space them according to the variety's requirements.

Example Planting Schedule:

- **Spring**: Start seeds indoors 6-8 weeks before the last frost. Transplant seedlings outdoors after the danger of frost has passed.

- **Fall**: Direct sow hardy herbs like parsley and cilantro outdoors.

Caring for Your Medicinal Herb Garden

Benefits: Proper care ensures healthy plants that produce high-quality herbs for your use. It also helps prevent pests and diseases that can affect plant health.

How to Care:

- **Watering**: Keep soil consistently moist but not waterlogged. Water early in the day to prevent fungal issues.

- **Fertilizing**: Use organic fertilizers or compost to provide essential nutrients. Avoid over-fertilizing, which can affect herb quality.

- **Pruning**: Regularly trim herbs to encourage bushier growth and prevent them from becoming leggy. Remove spent flowers to prolong the harvest period.

- **Pest and Disease Control**: Monitor for common pests like aphids and spider mites. Use organic pest control methods such as neem oil or insecticidal soap if needed.

Example Maintenance Tasks:

- **Weeding**: Regularly remove weeds to reduce competition for nutrients and water.

- **Mulching**: Apply mulch to retain soil moisture and suppress weeds.

Harvesting and Using Medicinal Herbs

Benefits: Proper harvesting ensures you get the most potent and effective herbs. Using fresh or dried herbs from your garden can enhance your health and well-being.

How to Harvest:

- **Timing**: Harvest herbs when they are at their peak potency, usually just before they flower. For most herbs, this is in the morning after the dew has dried.

- **Method**: Use clean, sharp scissors or garden shears to cut stems. For leafy herbs, trim leaves from the top to encourage new growth.

Example Harvesting Techniques:

- **Leaves**: Harvest leaves individually or cut entire stems. For herbs like basil, regularly pinching back the top promotes fuller growth.

- **Flowers**: Harvest flowers when they are fully open but before they start to wilt. Dry flowers carefully to preserve their medicinal properties.

Drying and Storing Herbs:

- **Drying**: Hang herbs in small bundles in a dry, well-ventilated area away from direct sunlight. Alternatively, use a food dehydrator or oven on a low setting.

- **Storing**: Store dried herbs in airtight containers away from light and moisture. Label containers with the herb name and harvest date.

Example Herbal Remedies from Your Garden

Herbal Tea: Use dried herbs like chamomile, mint, or lemon balm to brew soothing herbal teas.

Herbal Infusions: Infuse herbs like calendula or lavender in oils for use in skin care or massage.

Herbal Salves: Create salves by infusing herbs like calendula or comfrey in oils and mixing with beeswax.

Conclusion

Growing your own medicinal herb garden is a fulfilling way to take control of your health and connect with nature. By planning carefully, providing proper care, and using your herbs thoughtfully, you can enjoy the many benefits of fresh, natural remedies. Start your herbal garden today and experience the satisfaction of nurturing plants that support your well-being.

Advanced Herbal Practices

Understanding Dosage and Potency

Understanding dosage and potency is crucial in the effective and safe use of herbal remedies. Proper dosing ensures that herbs provide their intended therapeutic benefits without causing adverse effects. Potency, or the strength of an herb's active compounds, can vary significantly, influencing how an herb should be used.

Key Concepts

1. Potency

- **Definition**: Potency refers to the strength or concentration of an herb's active compounds that contribute to its therapeutic effects. This can be influenced by factors such as the plant's growing conditions, the part of the plant used, and the preparation method.

- **Variability**: Potency can vary between different batches of herbs due to differences in soil, climate, and harvesting times. This variability can affect the consistency of herbal treatments.

2. Dosage

- **Definition**: Dosage is the amount of an herb used to achieve a specific therapeutic effect. It can be influenced by factors such as the herb's potency, the individual's health condition, age, weight, and overall health.

- **Forms of Herbal Remedies**: Dosage guidelines differ depending on the form of the herb—whether it's used as a tea, tincture, capsule, or topical application.

Determining Dosage

1. Herb Forms and Dosages

- **Herbal Teas**: Typically made from dried herbs steeped in hot water. Common dosages are 1-2 teaspoons of dried herb per cup of water. Drink 2-3 cups daily, but adjustments may be needed based on the herb and individual response.

- **Tinctures**: Alcohol-based extracts that are more concentrated. Standard dosages often range from 1-2 dropperfuls (30-60 drops) 2-3 times daily. Dosage can be adjusted according to the potency of the tincture and the individual's needs.

- **Capsules/Tablets**: Contain powdered herb or extracts. Follow manufacturer guidelines or consult an herbalist for dosage recommendations based on the concentration and purpose of the herb.

- **Topicals**: Include salves, oils, and ointments applied directly to the skin. Dosage is less standardized but generally involves applying a small amount to the affected area 1-3 times daily.

2. Calculating Dosage

- **Standardized Extracts**: Many commercial herbal products are standardized to contain a specific percentage of active compounds. Standardized extracts help ensure consistency in dosage and potency.

- **Individual Factors**: Adjust dosage based on individual factors such as age, weight, overall health, and concurrent medications. For example, children and elderly individuals may require lower dosages.

3. Adjusting Dosage

- **Start Low and Go Slow**: Begin with the lower end of the dosage range and gradually increase as needed, monitoring for efficacy and any adverse effects.

- **Monitor Effects**: Pay attention to how your body responds to the herb. Adjust the dosage based on therapeutic effects and any side effects experienced.

Potency Considerations

1. Preparation Methods

- **Infusions**: Steeping herbs in hot water can extract certain compounds but may not be as potent as other methods like tincturing.

- **Decoctions**: Boiling herbs in water extracts compounds that are not easily released through simple infusions, such as roots and bark.

- **Tinctures**: Alcohol-based extractions concentrate the herb's active compounds and can be more potent than teas or infusions.

- **Powdered Herbs**: When used in capsules or as a powder, potency depends on the quality and concentration of the herb.

2. Factors Affecting Potency

- **Growing Conditions**: Soil quality, climate, and harvesting time can influence the concentration of active compounds in herbs.

- **Processing and Storage**: Proper processing (e.g., drying, grinding) and storage (e.g., airtight containers, away from light) help maintain potency. Exposure to air, moisture, and light can degrade active compounds.

Practical Tips

1. Documentation: Keep detailed records of the herbs used, their forms, dosages, and any effects experienced. This helps track efficacy and make informed adjustments.

2. Consultation: Work with a qualified herbalist or healthcare provider to tailor dosage and potency recommendations based on individual health needs and conditions.

3. Education: Continuously educate yourself on new research and guidelines related to herbal medicine to stay informed about best practices for dosage and potency.

Conclusion

Understanding dosage and potency is essential for the effective and safe use of herbal remedies. By considering factors such as the form of the herb, individual health conditions, and preparation methods, you can optimize the therapeutic benefits of herbal treatments. Start with lower doses, adjust as needed, and consult with experts to ensure that your herbal practices are both effective and safe.

Personalized Herbal Protocols: Tailoring Remedies to Your Needs

Personalized herbal protocols are customized plans designed to address individual health conditions, goals, and needs through the use of herbal remedies. Tailoring herbal treatments ensures that they are effective and suited to the individual's unique circumstances, enhancing their therapeutic benefits and minimizing potential side effects.

Steps to Develop Personalized Herbal Protocols

1. Assessing Health Conditions

Benefits: A thorough assessment helps identify the root causes of health issues and informs the selection of appropriate herbs and remedies. Understanding individual health conditions allows for more targeted and effective treatment.

How to Assess Health Conditions:

- **Medical History**: Review the individual's medical history, including chronic conditions, past illnesses, surgeries, and family health history.

- **Current Symptoms**: Document current symptoms, their frequency, severity, and any patterns or triggers.

- **Medications and Supplements**: List all medications and supplements being taken to identify potential interactions with herbs.

- **Lifestyle Factors**: Consider lifestyle factors such as diet, stress levels, sleep patterns, and physical activity.

Example Assessment:

- **Chronic Stress**: An individual experiencing high levels of stress might benefit from adaptogenic herbs like ashwagandha and rhodiola, combined with calming herbs like chamomile and lemon balm.

2. Identifying Health Goals

Benefits: Defining specific health goals helps focus the herbal protocol on achieving desired outcomes, whether they are related to symptom relief, overall wellness, or preventive care.

How to Identify Health Goals:

- **Short-Term Goals**: These might include alleviating specific symptoms or managing acute health issues.

- **Long-Term Goals**: Focus on overall health improvements, such as boosting immunity, supporting digestive health, or reducing chronic inflammation.

Example Goals:

- **Boosting Immunity**: Goals might include reducing the frequency of colds and flu, improving energy levels, and enhancing overall immune function.

- **Improving Digestion**: Goals might include alleviating bloating, improving regularity, and reducing symptoms of digestive disorders.

3. Selecting Herbs

Benefits: Choosing the right herbs based on their therapeutic properties and compatibility with individual needs enhances the effectiveness of the herbal protocol.

How to Select Herbs:

- **Research Herb Properties**: Study the therapeutic effects, benefits, and potential side effects of different herbs.

- **Match Herbs to Needs**: Choose herbs that align with the individual's health goals and conditions. Consider factors such as the herb's action (e.g., anti-inflammatory, antimicrobial, adaptogenic) and its safety profile.
- **Consider Interactions**: Ensure that selected herbs do not interact negatively with any medications or other supplements the individual is taking.

Example Herb Selection:

- **For Anxiety**: Herbs such as valerian root, passionflower, and kava may be selected for their calming and anxiety-reducing effects.
- **For Joint Pain**: Herbs like turmeric, ginger, and willow bark may be chosen for their anti-inflammatory and pain-relieving properties.

4. Creating the Protocol

Benefits: Developing a detailed protocol ensures that the herbs are used effectively and consistently, optimizing their therapeutic benefits.

How to Create the Protocol:

- **Dosage**: Determine appropriate dosages based on the form of the herb (e.g., tea, tincture, capsule) and individual requirements.
- **Frequency**: Establish how often the herbs should be taken, such as daily or several times a week.
- **Duration**: Set a timeframe for using the herbs, including any necessary adjustments based on progress and response.

Example Protocol:

- **Stress Management**: A protocol might include 1 cup of chamomile tea in the evening for relaxation, 2 dropperfuls of ashwagandha tincture daily for stress resilience, and 1 capsule of rhodiola in the morning to support energy levels.

5. Monitoring and Adjusting

Benefits: Regular monitoring and adjustments help assess the effectiveness of the herbal protocol and make necessary changes to optimize results and address any side effects.

How to Monitor and Adjust:

- **Track Symptoms**: Keep a journal of symptoms, improvements, and any adverse effects experienced while using the herbal remedies.

- **Evaluate Progress**: Assess progress towards health goals and make adjustments to the protocol as needed.

- **Consultation**: Regularly consult with a healthcare provider or herbalist to review the protocol and make informed adjustments based on feedback and observations.

Example Monitoring:

- **Adjustment for Digestive Health**: If initial herbs for digestion are not effective, consider adjusting dosages, adding new herbs, or exploring potential food sensitivities.

Conclusion

Personalized herbal protocols involve a thoughtful approach to addressing individual health needs through customized herbal treatments. By assessing health conditions, identifying goals, selecting appropriate herbs, creating a detailed protocol, and monitoring progress, you can tailor herbal remedies to achieve optimal results. Consulting with qualified herbalists or healthcare providers can further enhance the effectiveness and safety of personalized herbal protocols.

Working with a Holistic Health Practitioner

Collaborating with a holistic health practitioner can greatly enhance the effectiveness of your personalized herbal protocol and overall health journey. Holistic practitioners take a comprehensive approach to health, considering the physical, emotional, mental, and spiritual aspects of well-being. They can provide personalized advice, help integrate herbal remedies with other therapeutic modalities, and offer ongoing support.

Benefits of Working with a Holistic Health Practitioner

1. Comprehensive Assessment

- **Holistic Perspective**: Practitioners consider your overall health, including physical symptoms, emotional state, lifestyle, and environmental factors. This comprehensive view helps in creating a more effective and balanced treatment plan.

- **Personalized Recommendations**: They can tailor herbal remedies and other treatments to your specific needs, ensuring that all aspects of your health are addressed.

2. Expert Guidance

- **Herbal Expertise**: Holistic practitioners have in-depth knowledge of herbal medicine, including the properties, interactions, and proper use of various herbs.

- **Integrative Approach**: They can combine herbal remedies with other therapeutic modalities, such as nutrition, acupuncture, or mindfulness practices, for a more holistic approach to health.

3. Safety and Monitoring

- **Avoiding Interactions**: Practitioners can help you avoid potential interactions between herbs and any medications or supplements you may be taking.

- **Ongoing Support**: They provide regular check-ins to monitor your progress, adjust protocols as needed, and address any concerns or side effects.

Steps to Working with a Holistic Health Practitioner

1. Finding a Practitioner

- **Credentials**: Look for practitioners with relevant qualifications and certifications in holistic health, herbal medicine, or related fields. Common credentials include Licensed Acupuncturist (LAc), Certified Herbalist, or Doctor of Naturopathic Medicine (ND).

- **Referrals and Reviews**: Seek recommendations from friends, family, or healthcare providers, and read reviews to find a reputable practitioner with a good track record.

2. Initial Consultation

- **Preparation**: Prepare a comprehensive health history, including current symptoms, medications, supplements, and lifestyle factors. Be ready to discuss your health goals and any concerns you may have.

- **Assessment**: During the initial consultation, the practitioner will conduct a thorough assessment, which may include a review of your medical history, physical examination, and possibly diagnostic tests.

3. Developing a Plan

- **Customized Protocol**: Based on the assessment, the practitioner will create a personalized herbal protocol and may recommend additional therapies or lifestyle changes.

- **Goals and Expectations**: Discuss your health goals and set realistic expectations for the protocol. Understand the duration of the treatment, expected outcomes, and any potential side effects.

4. Implementing the Plan

- **Follow Instructions**: Adhere to the practitioner's recommendations regarding herbal dosages, frequency, and any additional treatments or lifestyle changes.

- **Track Progress**: Keep a record of your symptoms, any improvements, and any side effects. This information will be valuable for future consultations.

5. Ongoing Support and Adjustments

- **Regular Check-ins**: Schedule follow-up appointments to review your progress, discuss any issues, and make necessary adjustments to the protocol.

- **Communication**: Maintain open communication with your practitioner to address any questions or concerns that arise during the treatment.

6. Integrating Additional Therapies

- **Complementary Modalities**: If recommended, integrate other therapies such as nutritional counseling, acupuncture, or mindfulness practices into your health plan for a more holistic approach.

Common Therapies Used by Holistic Practitioners

1. Herbal Medicine

- **Custom Blends**: Personalized herbal blends tailored to your specific health needs.

- **Formulations**: Various forms including teas, tinctures, capsules, and topical applications.

2. Nutrition and Diet

- **Dietary Recommendations**: Guidance on nutrition and dietary changes to support overall health and enhance the effectiveness of herbal remedies.

3. Acupuncture

- **Energy Balance**: Techniques to balance energy flow and support healing.

4. Mindfulness and Stress Management

- **Techniques**: Practices such as meditation, yoga, and breathing exercises to reduce stress and improve mental well-being.

Conclusion

Working with a holistic health practitioner offers a comprehensive and personalized approach to health management. Their expertise in herbal medicine, combined with a holistic perspective, ensures that your treatment plan addresses all aspects of your well-being. By finding a qualified practitioner, engaging in thorough assessments, and following a customized protocol, you can enhance your health journey and achieve better outcomes with herbal remedies and other complementary therapies.

Ethical Considerations in Wildcrafting and Using Herbs

Wildcrafting, the practice of foraging wild plants for medicinal and culinary use, requires careful attention to ethical and sustainable practices. Using herbs responsibly ensures the preservation of plant species, ecosystems, and the environment, while respecting local regulations and cultural practices. Ethical wildcrafting practices also help maintain the quality and potency of the herbs you collect.

Principles of Ethical Wildcrafting

1. Sustainability

Definition: Sustainability in wildcrafting involves harvesting plants in a way that ensures their continued growth and availability for future generations.

Practices:

- **Harvesting Limits**: Only take a small percentage of a plant population to avoid overharvesting. A general rule is to harvest no more than 10% of a plant population.

- **Timing**: Harvest at the right time for optimal potency and to avoid disrupting the plant's lifecycle. For example, collect leaves in spring and roots in fall.

- **Propagation**: Ensure that plants have a chance to reproduce before harvesting. Avoid disturbing young plants and seeds.

Example: When collecting echinacea, harvest only a few plants from a large population to ensure the species can continue to thrive in the wild.

2. Respect for Local Ecosystems

Definition: Respecting local ecosystems involves understanding and protecting the delicate balance of plant and animal life in their natural habitats.

Practices:

- **Avoid Disturbance**: Minimize environmental impact by avoiding sensitive areas and not trampling vegetation or soil.

- **Leave No Trace**: Clean up any tools or waste to prevent contamination and damage to the environment.

- **Protect Endangered Species**: Do not harvest plants that are endangered or protected by law.

Example: When foraging in a nature reserve, follow designated trails and avoid collecting plants in sensitive areas to protect the habitat.

3. Legal and Cultural Considerations

Definition: Adhering to local laws and respecting cultural traditions and rights related to plant use and wildcrafting.

Practices:

- **Obtain Permits**: Check and obtain any necessary permits for wildcrafting in public lands or protected areas.

- **Respect Indigenous Rights**: Recognize and honor the traditional knowledge and rights of indigenous peoples who have historical ties to the plants.

- **Follow Regulations**: Adhere to local and national regulations regarding the collection of wild plants.

Example: Before collecting herbs in a national park, ensure you have the required permits and follow park regulations to avoid legal issues.

4. Ethical Harvesting Techniques

Definition: Using harvesting techniques that ensure the plant's health and the longevity of its population.

Practices:

- **Selective Harvesting**: Choose mature plants and avoid harvesting rare or slow-growing species.

- **Tool Use**: Use clean, sharp tools to reduce damage to plants and avoid spreading diseases.

- **Replanting**: If possible, replant seeds or parts of the plant to support regeneration.

Example: When harvesting wild ginseng, dig carefully to avoid damaging the root system and replanting any seeds you collect to aid future growth.

5. Knowledge and Education

Definition: Continuously educating yourself about plants, their habitats, and the ethical practices of wildcrafting.

Practices:

- **Research**: Stay informed about the plants you collect, their ecological roles, and best practices for sustainable harvesting.

- **Training**: Seek training or mentorship from experienced wildcrafters or herbalists to enhance your skills and knowledge.

Example: Attend workshops or join local herbalist groups to learn about sustainable wildcrafting practices and share knowledge with others.

Conclusion

Ethical wildcrafting and the use of herbs require a commitment to sustainability, respect for local ecosystems, adherence to legal and cultural considerations, and the use of responsible harvesting techniques. By following these ethical principles, you can ensure that your wildcrafting practices contribute positively to the environment and communities, while preserving the quality and effectiveness of the herbs you collect.

Case Studies and Success Stories

Real-Life Experiences with Natural Healing

Real-life experiences with natural healing offer a glimpse into the transformative power of herbal remedies and holistic practices. These stories reflect personal journeys where individuals have turned to natural approaches to improve their health and well-being. By sharing these experiences, readers can gain inspiration and practical insights into how natural healing can be applied in various situations.

Experience 1: Conquering Chronic Fatigue with Adaptogens

Background: Emily, a 45-year-old office worker, struggled with chronic fatigue and low energy levels for years. Despite trying various treatments, she found little relief and was looking for a natural solution.

Approach: Emily decided to explore adaptogens, herbs known for their ability to help the body adapt to stress and boost energy levels.

Process:

- **Adaptogen Supplementation**: Emily began taking ashwagandha and rhodiola supplements daily.

- **Lifestyle Changes**: She also incorporated regular exercise, improved her diet, and practiced mindfulness.

Outcome:

- **Increased Energy**: Within a few months, Emily reported a significant increase in energy levels and reduced feelings of fatigue.

- **Enhanced Resilience**: She felt better equipped to handle daily stressors and improve overall well-being.

Lesson Learned: Adaptogens like ashwagandha and rhodiola can play a crucial role in managing chronic fatigue, especially when combined with lifestyle changes.

Experience 2: Managing High Blood Pressure with Hawthorn

Background: David, a 60-year-old man with a history of high blood pressure, was concerned about the side effects of his prescription medication. He sought a natural alternative to manage his condition.

Approach: David turned to hawthorn, an herb traditionally used to support cardiovascular health and lower blood pressure.

Process:

- **Hawthorn Tea**: David started drinking hawthorn tea daily.

- **Supplementation**: He also used hawthorn extract capsules as a supplement.

Outcome:

- **Blood Pressure Reduction**: David experienced a noticeable decrease in his blood pressure readings over several months.

- **Improved Heart Health**: He reported feeling more comfortable with his cardiovascular health and experienced fewer side effects.

Lesson Learned: Hawthorn can be an effective natural remedy for managing high blood pressure, offering a valuable alternative to conventional medications.

Experience 3: Easing Digestive Issues with Peppermint

Background: Lisa, a 28-year-old woman, had long struggled with digestive issues, including bloating and gas. Conventional treatments provided minimal relief.

Approach: Lisa decided to try peppermint, an herb known for its soothing effects on the digestive system.

Process:

- **Peppermint Tea**: Lisa drank peppermint tea after meals to help with digestion.

- **Peppermint Oil**: She also used peppermint oil in a diluted form for abdominal massages.

Outcome:

- **Symptom Relief**: Lisa found significant relief from bloating and gas, and her digestion improved.

- **Comfort**: She was able to manage her digestive issues more effectively and comfortably.

Lesson Learned: Peppermint is a practical and effective remedy for digestive discomfort, providing relief and improved digestive function.

Experience 4: Supporting Mental Clarity with Ginkgo Biloba

Background: Robert, a 50-year-old academic, was experiencing cognitive decline and memory issues. He wanted to explore natural options to support mental clarity and cognitive function.

Approach: Robert began using ginkgo biloba, an herb known for its potential cognitive benefits and memory support.

Process:

- **Ginkgo Supplements**: Robert took ginkgo biloba supplements daily as recommended.
- **Cognitive Practices**: He also engaged in mental exercises and a balanced diet to support cognitive health.

Outcome:

- **Enhanced Focus**: Robert noticed improved mental clarity and better focus on tasks.
- **Memory Improvement**: He experienced some improvement in memory recall and cognitive function.

Lesson Learned: Ginkgo biloba can offer support for cognitive health and memory, especially when combined with other healthy lifestyle practices.

Experience 5: Treating Insomnia with Valerian Root

Background: Jessica, a 37-year-old professional, struggled with chronic insomnia and found it difficult to fall asleep without medication. She wanted a natural solution for better sleep.

Approach: Jessica turned to valerian root, an herb traditionally used to promote relaxation and improve sleep quality.

Process:

- **Valerian Root Tea**: Jessica drank valerian root tea before bedtime.
- **Supplementation**: She also used valerian root capsules for added effect.

Outcome:

- **Improved Sleep**: Jessica experienced improved sleep quality and found it easier to fall asleep.

- **Reduced Dependence**: She was able to reduce her reliance on prescription sleep aids.

Lesson Learned: Valerian root can be an effective natural remedy for insomnia, helping to improve sleep quality and reduce dependence on medications.

Conclusion

Real-life experiences with natural healing demonstrate the potential benefits of herbal remedies and holistic practices in addressing various health challenges. These stories highlight how individuals have successfully incorporated natural approaches into their lives, leading to improved health and well-being. By learning from these experiences, readers can gain practical insights and inspiration for exploring natural healing options in their own lives.

Overcoming Chronic Illness with Herbal Medicine

Chronic illnesses can be challenging to manage and often require a multifaceted approach to treatment. Herbal medicine offers a complementary path to conventional treatments, providing potential relief and improvement in quality of life. This section explores real-life examples of individuals who have successfully used herbal medicine to overcome or manage chronic illnesses, showcasing the potential benefits and practical applications of herbal remedies in chronic health conditions.

Case Study 1: Managing Rheumatoid Arthritis with Turmeric and Ginger

Background: Alice, a 55-year-old woman, was diagnosed with rheumatoid arthritis (RA) several years ago. The disease caused significant joint pain and stiffness, and conventional treatments were not fully effective.

Approach: Alice decided to incorporate turmeric and ginger, both known for their anti-inflammatory properties, into her regimen to manage her RA symptoms.

Process:

- **Turmeric Supplements**: Alice began taking 1,000 mg of turmeric daily, combined with black pepper to enhance absorption.

- **Ginger Tea**: She drank ginger tea twice a day.

Outcome:

- **Reduced Pain and Stiffness**: After a few months, Alice noticed a significant reduction in joint pain and stiffness.
- **Improved Mobility**: She experienced improved mobility and overall function.

Lesson Learned: Turmeric and ginger can be effective in managing chronic inflammatory conditions like rheumatoid arthritis, offering a natural approach to symptom relief.

Case Study 2: Alleviating Chronic Fatigue Syndrome with Ashwagandha and Rhodiola

Background: Michael, a 40-year-old man, had been suffering from chronic fatigue syndrome (CFS) for several years, leading to persistent exhaustion and reduced quality of life.

Approach: Michael turned to adaptogenic herbs as part of his strategy to address CFS. He used ashwagandha and rhodiola to help combat fatigue and improve energy levels.

Process:

- **Ashwagandha**: Michael took 300 mg of ashwagandha extract daily.
- **Rhodiola**: He also took 200 mg of rhodiola extract daily.

Outcome:

- **Increased Energy**: Michael reported increased energy levels and reduced fatigue after several weeks of consistent use.
- **Enhanced Well-Being**: His overall sense of well-being improved, and he was able to engage in daily activities more comfortably.

Lesson Learned: Adaptogens like ashwagandha and rhodiola can be beneficial in managing chronic fatigue syndrome by supporting energy levels and overall resilience.

Case Study 3: Supporting Diabetes Management with Cinnamon and Bitter Melon

Background: Priya, a 60-year-old woman, was diagnosed with type 2 diabetes. Despite following her prescribed medication regimen, she sought additional ways to manage her blood sugar levels naturally.

Approach: Priya incorporated cinnamon and bitter melon into her daily routine to support her diabetes management.

Process:

- **Cinnamon**: Priya added a teaspoon of ground cinnamon to her morning oatmeal and tea.

- **Bitter Melon**: She drank bitter melon juice and took bitter melon supplements.

Outcome:

- **Improved Blood Sugar Control**: Priya experienced better blood sugar control and reduced fluctuations in her glucose levels.

- **Overall Health**: She noticed improvements in her energy levels and overall health.

Lesson Learned: Cinnamon and bitter melon can support blood sugar management in individuals with type 2 diabetes, providing a complementary approach to conventional treatments.

Case Study 4: Managing High Blood Pressure with Hibiscus and Garlic

Background: John, a 62-year-old man, had high blood pressure that was difficult to control with medication alone. He sought natural ways to support his cardiovascular health.

Approach: John began using hibiscus tea and garlic supplements to help manage his blood pressure.

Process:

- **Hibiscus Tea**: John drank hibiscus tea twice a day.

- **Garlic Supplements**: He took garlic supplements daily.

Outcome:

- **Lowered Blood Pressure**: John observed a reduction in his blood pressure readings after incorporating these herbs.

- **Improved Cardiovascular Health**: He felt more confident in managing his cardiovascular health naturally.

Lesson Learned: Hibiscus and garlic can be effective in supporting cardiovascular health and managing high blood pressure, offering a natural complement to conventional treatments.

Case Study 5: Addressing Chronic Digestive Disorders with Slippery Elm and Marshmallow Root

Background: Linda, a 48-year-old woman, had been struggling with chronic digestive disorders, including irritable bowel syndrome (IBS) and chronic gastritis.

Approach: Linda explored slippery elm and marshmallow root as natural remedies to soothe and heal her digestive tract.

Process:

- **Slippery Elm Powder**: Linda took slippery elm powder mixed with water daily.

- **Marshmallow Root Tea**: She drank marshmallow root tea to help soothe her digestive lining.

Outcome:

- **Symptom Relief**: Linda experienced relief from digestive discomfort, including reduced inflammation and irritation.

- **Improved Digestive Health**: Her overall digestive health improved, leading to fewer symptoms and better quality of life.

Lesson Learned: Slippery elm and marshmallow root can be effective in managing chronic digestive disorders, providing soothing and healing effects on the digestive tract.

Conclusion

These real-life experiences illustrate how herbal medicine can complement conventional treatments and offer significant benefits for managing chronic illnesses. By incorporating herbal remedies thoughtfully and consistently, individuals have found relief and improved their overall quality of life. These stories underscore the potential of herbal medicine as a valuable tool in addressing chronic health conditions and enhancing well-being.

Conclusion

As we conclude this exploration into natural healing and herbal remedies, it is clear that the path to wellness is multifaceted and deeply personal. Natural remedies offer a valuable complement to conventional medical treatments, providing additional tools for managing health and enhancing overall well-being. This book has aimed to empower readers with knowledge and practical strategies to incorporate natural remedies into their daily lives.

Key Takeaways

1. **Integration of Tradition and Science**: The integration of traditional herbal wisdom with modern scientific research allows for a more comprehensive approach to health. Understanding the scientific basis behind herbal remedies helps in applying them effectively and safely.

2. **Herbal Synergies**: Combining herbs can enhance their therapeutic effects. Learning about herbal synergies and creating balanced blends can optimize the benefits of natural remedies and address a range of health issues more effectively.

3. **Practical Application**: Simple ingredients like garlic, ginger, and turmeric have proven significant impacts on health. Utilizing these common herbs and ingredients in everyday life can lead to improved health outcomes and well-being.

4. **Personalization and Safety**: Tailoring herbal protocols to individual needs and ensuring safety in herbal practices are crucial for achieving desired results. Consulting with holistic health practitioners and understanding dosage and potency can enhance the effectiveness of herbal remedies.

5. **Holistic Approach**: Incorporating natural remedies into a holistic lifestyle—including diet, self-care practices, and stress management—can lead to more profound and sustainable health improvements.

Encouragement for Continued Learning and Exploration

The journey toward natural wellness is ongoing. Continued learning about herbal remedies, their applications, and emerging research can enrich your understanding and practice. Engaging with communities of like-minded individuals, seeking guidance from experts, and staying informed about new developments in herbal medicine can support your path to health and well-being.

The Future of Natural Remedies in Modern Health Care

Natural remedies are increasingly recognized for their role in modern health care. As interest in integrative and holistic approaches grows, the integration of herbal medicine and natural remedies with conventional treatments holds promise for more comprehensive and personalized health care solutions.

By embracing natural healing and incorporating it thoughtfully into your lifestyle, you can take proactive steps toward achieving and maintaining optimal health. Remember that the power of natural remedies lies not only in the herbs themselves but also in the commitment to a balanced and informed approach to health.

Final Thoughts

Thank you for joining this journey into the world of natural healing and herbal medicine. May the knowledge and insights shared in this book inspire you to explore, experiment, and experience the benefits of natural remedies. Embrace the wisdom of nature and the power of herbal medicine as you continue your journey toward a healthier, more vibrant life.

Made in the USA
Middletown, DE
22 August 2024

59593900R00099